CHOOSING LOVE

Living Our Lives to Nourish Our Hearts

Meredith Gaston

Hardie Grant

BOOKS

CONTENTS

Dearest You

Between us there exists a tremendous force: an all-encompassing energy that quietly but surely embraces us and all things. It is our natural instinct, our point and purpose; it is profound and light all at once and has the power to achieve great things. It propels us forward at every turn, offering nourishment and inspiration. This energetic force — love — nurtures and connects, supports and defines us. Nothing can create quite the same joy and bliss, the same pain and grief, the same delight and pleasure, nor inspire the same degree of reverence, as love.

More than a feeling, love is an active and miraculous force. Love is the thread uniting the mysterious and resplendent patchwork of our shared lives and works in nuanced, serendipitous ways. As renewable energy, love transcends time and space. It motivates, comforts, heals and frees us. It connects us and allows us to feel a sense of belonging — to feel and know that we are part of something deeper, greater and more sacred than we could ever fully capture with words. Almost as if by nature, love defies snappy definition. Instead it dances with us — whispering through the portals of all our senses, infusing our imaginations and igniting our dreams.

Love encompasses so many things, from tenderness, compassion and courage, to warmth, grace and joy. Love is understanding, open and attentive. It is love that teaches, enlivens, challenges and nurtures us more profoundly than any other force on earth possibly could. And we love courageously and brilliantly, even in the face of so much mystery and uncertainty, because it is our natural instinct to do so. Because our hearts, minds and spirits are completely dynamic, interpreting and responding to life in every moment. We love because we are compelled to love, just as plants are compelled to grow into the light. We love because we are moved by beauty and the promise of joy. We love intuitively because connection is crucial for our wellbeing and survival, and because loving is unto itself a lifelong virtue — a reason for being. We love because, beyond all reason, logic and division, we are all sentient, emotional beings sharing an interwoven past, present and future.

All kinds of love exist between us. Family love and love within friendships. Romantic love, self-love, even great love: the blissful, ecstatic kind of love we feel in heightened moments of aliveness, in which we sense love for all life and creation. We can love our children, our pets, our favourite hobbies, or particular pieces of art. We can love certain places, songs or people that touch our hearts. We can feel moved by poems and stories that awaken our senses. Indeed, what we love, who and how we love are indicative of our deepest, innermost values and desires. Our different ways of feeling, giving and receiving love demonstrate who we are and guide us as we create meaningful lives expressive of our natures and dreams.

When we tune into the energy of love, as if dipping into a particular pool of thought and feeling, we are the recipients of infinite vital energy.

With this loving energy, we can shift our perspective, transform ourselves personally, and change our shared world in the most magnificent and positive ways. Tuning into love, we may transform our fears into challenges to meet and triumphantly overcome. We can learn to flourish through good times and hard times, forgive and let go, even thrive amid change and uncertainty. We all contend with moments of light- and heavy-heartedness as we navigate our busy, nuanced daily lives. All the while, and even in our trickiest, most trying moments, love exists and pulsates as healing, fortifying energy. Cultivating love brings bliss and meaning to our lives. As we attune ourselves to love, we feel its constant magic working within and around us. We need only see and choose love for it to reveal itself as our most faithful, constant companion — our brightest guiding light.

Choosing love is becoming increasingly important in our rapidly changing world. So much has shifted all around us, and our lives are vastly accelerated and more overstimulating than ever before. All the while, our essential human design remains the same. Our nervous systems are constantly striving to adjust to navigate the demands of modern daily life. It is no wonder that we can often feel anxious, separate, unloving or unloved. That we can feel worn out, hurried, suspicious, confused and lonely. That we are more connected yet feel so disconnected. That we don't know when to let go and when to hold on. Amid much noise we often can't quite hear our hearts and, as a result, can stand in our very own way when it comes to love. It is no surprise that the state of our hearts warrants our special attention, time and care right now.

> Life is calling us to live more lovingly, harmoniously and compassionately than ever before.

Choosing love, we can return to community- and kin-centred living. We can identify that separateness, competition and loneliness are detrimental to our health and happiness, and we can open our hearts to connection and togetherness. While we are all individuals and our individuality is essential, we cannot survive and flourish with our personal interests at the heart of our thinking. While the concerns we face are complex and varied, the answer for all of us is one and the same. Quite simply, we must choose the way of love: a way of unity, peace and joy.

Love brings out the best in each and every one of us. Love is ours to feel, grow and share, if we wish to enjoy our lives and change the world. Love is ours for today, not tomorrow or some time yet to come. If we wish to live fully and embrace our aliveness with passion, we must open our hearts and minds. We must choose love.

Let us recognise love as the lifelong beacon for which we are searching. Let us notice that love is, and has always been, all around us, and that love dwells in our very own hearts and hands. When so many things can be chosen in this life, let us see and choose love.

Imagine our world rotating on an axis of love, each one of us choosing love for ourselves and one another. If such a peaceful, rich and kind world seems unrealistic, impossible, or even like a dream, philosopher and poet Henry David Thoreau can readily remind us that 'Our truest lives are when we are in dreams awake'. If anything can make the impossible possible, it is love. We must continue to dream, and nurture genuinely loving intentions for ourselves, each other and our earth.

Let us explore love now. Let us take the time to replenish our hearts and listen to them very carefully. Let us discover greater balance and meaningful purpose through living lovingly, letting love light us up and guide our way.

May this book encourage us all to nurture and open our hearts.

Meredith x

ENJOYING THIS BOOK

This decadent and abundant book about love has been written for everybody. For those younger, older and in between, for lovers and dreamers, for those feeling heartbroken, for parents and children, for deep thinkers, true romantics and passionate change makers.

Love touches us all, surrounding and enlivening us. Invisible love is constantly teaching and tickling us, imbuing us with strength, wisdom, comfort and joy. Indeed, love is a sea of energy in which we all flow — a way of life to which we all belong, and into which we are all welcomed.

This book is composed of twenty chapters on love, spanning concepts of wellbeing, intimacy and inspiration; creativity, beauty and courage; grief, loss, divine love and changing our world. At the end of each chapter you will discover a 'conversation with the heart'. At best, these conversations will be prompts for longer talks of your own design: private meetings with your own heart in which anything and everything can be shared.

Like beautiful prayers or meditations, these intimate conversations are wonderful resources that honour and rejuvenate our hearts. It may be that we have never spoken with our hearts before, and that initiating such conversations might initially feel a little unusual. Yet before too long we discover our hearts to be wonderful conversationalists, as well as the most constant, wise and loyal companions we could ever wish for. And what a treat this is.

Learning more about love allows us to learn more about ourselves and the mysteries of life. As a portal to the infinite wonders of life and our human experience on earth, love is a most worthy and wonderful subject. Exploring love opens doors to deepened bliss and insight, helping us on our way as we choose to lead bountiful, rich and meaningful lives.

I hope you will sink into these words and pictures, enjoying them in any way or sequence you please. I hope you will lay your hurries and worries down for these pages to absorb, transform and return to you with love. May the enchantment and inspiration of love touch you at the turn of every page, encouraging you to see and feel the magic and beauty of life. May you feel comforted, strengthened and encouraged as you move forward. Now let us begin.

I. HAVING A HEART

Our hearts beat with the very rhythm of our aliveness. While we don't often think about our physical hearts doing their tremendous work, it is thanks to them that life is circulated about our bodies, and that we are able to live and savour our busy, bountiful earthly days. The motif of a heart, and indeed our physical hearts themselves, have become synonymous with feeling and expressing love. Having 'feeling' hearts speaks to our human sensitivity, compassion and openness. While experiencing tenderness and a sense of connection through feeling love is not unique to our species, it seems that the human quality of our hearts — their inclinations and expressions — define, guide and inspire our lives. We live our lives to the fullest when we follow our hearts, embrace life wholeheartedly, and replenish our hearts by giving and receiving love.

Our physical hearts have become very important reference points in our bodies: epicentres of feeling and aliveness. When we make a pledge we place a hand over our heart. We talk about listening to or following our hearts as ways to express that we are taking heed of our innermost feelings and desires, being true to ourselves. When we hug one another we meet in a way that brings our physical hearts closer together, and when we have a conversation in which we really listen to each other we have a 'heart to heart'. We can 'wear our heart on our sleeve' or know things we care about 'off by heart'. We can feel heartened, broken-hearted, heavy-hearted or open-hearted. It is no coincidence that without a beating heart, we cannot live. For this and many other reasons, I tend to believe that love, like our very own hearts, is a life force completely essential to living, and one that in great part constitutes life itself.

Having feeling hearts means that things naturally move and inspire us in daily life, evoking our wonder and sensitivity, and touching us with joy, insight and inspiration. The overwhelming feeling of connection and elation we can experience looking into the eyes of someone dear to us reminds us why we love. The life-affirming, invigorating splendour of a spectacular view, the sublime inspiration of a piece of art or music that can move us in a way we perhaps cannot quite explain – these experiences speak to our knowingness of love. The extreme deliciousness and magnitude of love can render us speechless and bring us to tears, for sensing love inspires an immensity of feeling for which we all innately yearn.

We live in a time in which machinery and artificial intelligence can replace human beings in various capacities. While clever and functional, these heartless substitutes for human beings simply cannot offer our spontaneity, lightness and candour. Indeed, it is our propensity for creative flexibility, our joyous idiosyncrasies, the levity of our humour, and our heartfelt, effusive warmth that exemplify precious, human qualities of love.

These human qualities of love, when cultivated and shared, bring a uniquely precious, enriching essence to life and living.

In the beautiful story *The Wizard of Oz*, Tin Man serenades the universe with a wonderful song. An empty vessel made of tin, he longs for a heart with which to feel – to be human and to 'really feel the part'. He sings about all the things he could do, if only he had a heart, such as be tender, gentle and sentimental; take pleasure in love and art, befriend sparrows and even boys shooting arrows. As we listen, we are reminded what a gift it is to have a heart. What a privilege it is to be alive, and to live with the propensity to drink life in fully and deeply.

To really care for our hearts, it is essential that we make time to replenish them each day. There are infinite ways in which we can do this, building heart-centred daily lives in which we may feel truly satisfied and nourished.

We can begin by living honestly and lovingly, with compassion and integrity. We can commit to knowing and caring for ourselves unconditionally as we grow and change over time. We can practise expanding love through nurturing self-care practices. We can follow our passions and embrace our creativity to bring joy to our hearts. We can foster respectful, positive relationships in which we celebrate ourselves and enjoy those with whom we share our lives. In these and many other wonderful ways, we can learn to connect with our hearts, loving and exploring them in daily life.

As we choose to live lovingly, we begin to recognise endless opportunities and reasons to commune with ourselves and experience the compelling aliveness of our own complete presence here and now — a wholehearted physical, emotional and spiritual experience of life.

Dear Heart

It could be quite a while since we last spoke.

This might even be my very first conversation with you.

In any case, I would like to offer you my gratitude
for the energy you move about my body day and night,
and for the sheer miracle of my aliveness.

You keep a beat for me and I needn't even ask.
You navigate my feelings and awaken me to love.

For all the times I have followed you and found my happiness,
I feel thankful.

For all the times you have hurt and I haven't known how to nurture you,
I am here for you now.

For the things you tell me so clearly without words
and for the language of my emotions,
I give thanks.

I notice that before thinking, I feel.
May I feel in love and truth
so that I may always know my best way forward.

Thank you for listening, Heart.
Speak soon.

2. FEELING LOVE

Feeling love is a way of life, a gift, a necessity, and in itself a reason for being. To feel love is a tremendously powerful and active experience of sensing and expressing, giving and receiving energy. Albeit a natural thing, to love and be loved can take great faith, courage and patience at times. Indeed, while feeling love brings us deep comfort and joy, it can make us vulnerable to feeling deep hurt, disappointment and sadness too. All the while, we feel instinctively drawn to love's promise of beauty, enlightenment, meaning and bliss — loving without always knowing how or why. In this way, the miracle of love and our personal experiences of it enchant, illuminate and awaken us. In the exquisite words of Helen Keller, 'The best and most beautiful things in the world cannot be seen or even touched — they must be felt with the heart.'

Love has many faces and is experienced in deeply intimate, nuanced ways. In the English language we seem to draw upon one word for love. In other languages, such as ancient Greek, there are many different words for love. These words more specifically capture the depth and breadth of love: passion, affection, selflessness, familial love, obsessiveness, playfulness, enduring love and self-love. We can love life and love one another, love our children, ourselves, our pets and our homes – even places and spaces that touch our hearts. We can feel love for relative strangers in fleeting moments, and for our loved ones in spirit. We can experience love in a romantic sense, or savour sustaining love within our friendships. We can even connect with a great, timeless and ecstatic energy of love, emerging from a profound sense of interconnectedness with all life. Indeed, love is so grand that to list its many faces and expressions would be a sublime but endless pursuit. In its infinite forms, however, love has a signature effect upon us – love uplifts and fortifies us, replenishing our hearts.

Feeling love is an organic, visceral thing. It imbues our bodies with energy, comfort and vitality. The nurturing and refreshing qualities of love heighten our spirits and our thoughts. Love lightens our steps through the world and elevates the ways in which we interact with others. Love softens our gaze and our speech, ruffles our hard edges and opens us up to the beauty and fullness of life. Indeed, through loving eyes, our world becomes infinitely more beautiful. To live our lives attuned to love, with open hearts and minds, guarantees us truly joyous and abundant journeys. Living lovingly gifts us with feelings, connections and experiences to sustain and inspire us.

To feel loved is to know the peace of being understood and treasured as we are. It is to be seen and appreciated sincerely and fully, and to be met in all our imperfectly perfect human splendour. To feel loved strengthens, unites and relaxes us. It enhances our sense of wellbeing by amplifying our vitality, contentment and creativity. It helps us to acknowledge ourselves more lovingly, too: seeing ourselves through others' loving eyes, we may come to flourish in our own tenderness.

With our love, we can make ourselves and others feel very special. To love ourselves and each other is to cultivate happiness and demonstrate the power of our care. It is to want the best for ourselves, others and the environments in which we live, and to put effort into nurturing and honouring what exists there. To love is to make someone or something feel all the more rich and beautiful with our attention and affection. With love for ourselves and each other, we can ease and lighten life on earth. We take joy in each other's joy, celebrate our differences and successes, and make quality time to nurture and understand one another. By choosing love each day, we grow and share much-needed kindness and peace on earth.

Feeling love begins within us. Our own personal wellspring of love is nourished by self-compassion and time spent within. When we choose to love and take care of ourselves in daily life, we nourish and expand the energy of love within us. We fill our cups of love so that they may overflow to delight others in our lives. In this way, the love that dwells within us is the source of all other love we will ever come to see and know.

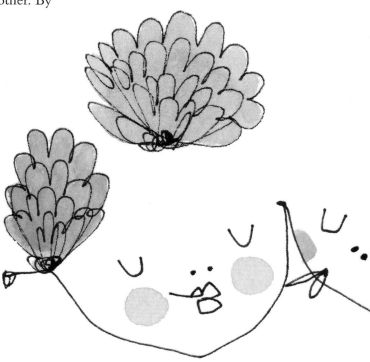

Being brave enough to embrace
love, even in the face of
impermanence and uncertainty,
enriches our life stories and our
spirits. It is by loving that we
live the full gamut of earthly and
heavenly feelings, exploring the
heights and depths of our humanity,
and leaving as few stones as possible
unturned on our paths. Embracing
life with love allows us to feel, and
it is in feeling that we come alive –
that we may relate compassionately,
live lusciously, and, ultimately, come
to know the innate beauty and
lightness of being.

Dear Heart

What a joy it is to feel love.

What a treat it is to know that I am thought of
and cared for,
not only by those I see and know,
but by heavenly love around and within me.

What bliss it is to feel the warmth
of tenderness and affection
and to nestle into the comfort of love.

Thank you, Heart,
for affording me such pleasure.

In all the moments in which I feel far from you,
help me to find you sparkling within me
sustaining and encouraging me,
helping me on my way.

At times in which I feel like a novice,
as if I am learning everything about love for the very first time,
grace me with the confidence and inner peace
I so deeply long to feel.

Ease my path forward
as I ease into you,
and allow me to sense
the lightness and strength of love.

Dear Heart, in your infinite wisdom,
teach me love for myself and others.
Teach me to love life all the more each day
so that I may be truly enriched
by the joy and depth of feeling.

3. ANCHOR OF LOVE

There are wonderful advantages of having an 'anchor' in daily life — a philosophy, point and purpose to which we may constantly realign ourselves for strength, support and direction. In any moment — joyous, trying or otherwise — our anchor can help us to find balance again by offering much-needed clarity and comfort. Choosing love as our anchor in daily life is virtuous and courageous, exciting and empowering. Venturing out with anchors of love enables us to navigate our life with zest, compassion and grace. It also invites tremendous magic into our lives by virtue of the serendipity and happiness that loving energy always brings.

Choosing love can be easy when things are going smoothly – when we can more readily see the beauty in things, when our mood is light and our company is joyous. Choosing love becomes much harder in the face of unkindness, exhaustion, trepidation and frustration. Indeed, our emotions can pull us from pillar to post and, when left unattended, complicate the course of our lives. It is powerful to see that with a personal foundation of love cultivated within ourselves through daily self-care, we are better equipped emotionally to handle the inevitable ebbs and flows of life with greater insight and resilience. We needn't be all-consumed by the heavy or difficult feelings we face when we have love as our anchor – a timeless resource that constantly and simply docks us back into perspective and peace.

Choosing love and realigning ourselves with it moment to moment affords us deep learning. We may not understand others' thoughts and actions, especially the most distressing and unthinkable behaviours and acts we sense and see around us. It is natural that we feel saddened, even demoralised, by the magnitude of injustice and pain on earth. Yet, if we desire to be the change we wish to see in the world, we must exercise our non-judgement and compassion, expressing our willingness to listen and understand other people and their motivations, and see another view or way of being. In doing so, we realign ourselves with loving energy. While we may not have the answers, nor be able to make the immediate changes we wish to see at the scale we desire, we must begin by choosing and growing love ourselves.

We can call upon our anchors of love to ground us during difficult times, asking for the courage to forgive when we have been wronged, for extra faith when our reserves feel diminished, even for tenderness and companionship in our loneliness. We may also recognise love in the more buoyant and beautiful moments in our lives – times in which our joy flows freely. In such moments it is a wonderful practice to feel ourselves anchoring back into love with gratitude, sensing the calm and comfort that await us as we return home to our hearts.

Philosopher Marcus Aurelius taught that very little is needed to make a happy life – that a happy life is within us and our way of thinking. Choosing to think, see and act with love positively transforms our views and experiences of ourselves, others, our circumstances and surroundings. We can choose love as a joyous lens through which to see life, or as a light to illuminate our path. When facing fear, judgement, exclusion, and indeed any kind of challenge, we may anchor ourselves in love, bringing peace to others as we ourselves grow and flourish.

Love is an all-knowing, all-sensing energy that fills gaps, eases pain and works miracles within and around us. Love weaves magic into the patchworks of our lives. Each time we anchor ourselves in love we may sense ourselves settling back in, returning to the embrace of an energy so soothing, powerful and all-encompassing that we may surrender all manner of things too big or unknown to it. This simple, humble practice affords our hearts a depth of peace we intuitively know exists beyond any doubt – the bliss for which we so deeply yearn.

Dear Heart

I am blessed to have you
and to know you.

I feel safe just sensing
you are there for me
as a guiding light
and a living symbol of love.

The love that dwells within you
is the light of my spirit.

Help me to share my light
freely and generously
so I may spread love and joy
wherever I go.

When I am tested,
please light my path.
Help me to find my feet
and keep my faith in love.

When I am inspired,
fill me all the more.
Let my creativity
sing of my gratitude.

Dear Heart,
your happiness is very important to me.
Please help me to take care of you,
so that you may feel at peace.

If there is anything I need to know,
or anything you would like me to see,
please know that I am listening.

Thank you, and bye for now.

4. LOVE AND LEARNING

Love is divine work in progress. Like a fire that needs kindling and stoking to glow, or a garden that requires attention, time and care to thrive, love is never 'done' — love is alive. It is vital and ever changing, and, if we allow it, love can feel forever new. We cannot fully grasp love, and this exquisite realisation must be one of its greatest, most profound delights. Compelling and alluring as it is to fully understand and know something — sense with some degree of comfort and assuredness its edges and boundaries — love teases us with glimpses of itself. Love leaves infinitely more unseen than seen, floating in the realms of heaven and imagination, and felt in potent stirrings of our hearts, minds and spirits. We can, however, learn to love better. To love more fully and deeply. To kneel humbly at the altar of love while acting gallantly, kindly, as best and as bravely as we can. We may all endeavour, and, endeavouring in earnest, live in love.

How can we learn to love ourselves, each other and life more deeply? It takes courage to ask such a question, and willingness to take heed of the answers that are always and already dwelling within us. Indeed, the place to start is always within, as our love and care for ourselves sets the tone for our love and care for all others. When we learn to respect and care for ourselves with unconditional love, loving and caring for others with the same integrity and grace becomes very natural. Moreover, a willingness to heal any lingering, unsettling grievances or outworn, self-limiting beliefs about ourselves, love and life allows us to move forward in peace and joy. All relationships that we enjoy in our lives benefit most profoundly from the relationship that we nurture with ourselves. Shining light upon the areas within and around us that need our love, and tending to those areas with sensitivity and care, is profound emotional intelligence. It enables us to create lives that feel satisfying, full and free.

Learning to love more deeply involves a deeper dive into life. It involves exploring ourselves and the experience of being alive with bravery and curiosity, gratitude and wonder. We become more deeply acquainted with love as we open our hearts and minds to ourselves and each other, resisting the urge to judge, control and perfect things. Rather, we may choose to be open to new possibilities and avenues beyond those with which we are already familiar.

At times we may think, speak or act lovelessly, clumsily, or out of alignment with our innermost values. We abandon our foundation of love. In such moments it is no wonder that we feel rudderless and all at sea. Indeed, our careless, unloving ways deplete and sadden ourselves first and foremost, creating ripple effects that we can never quite fully see or know. Thankfully, consciously realigning ourselves with love in any moment offers us the power and means to replenish and sustain our hearts. We are granted infinite chances to try again and learn through love, as love is an infinite, renewable, forgiving and unconditional energy. Love – pure and light – awaits our acknowledgement and invitation at every turn. Inviting love to light our path forward allows us to lead empowered, relaxing and wonderful lives.

If we seek to learn more about love, we must learn to give and receive love gracefully. In giving and receiving love, expressing ourselves and listening carefully, we become more attuned to ourselves, each other and the worlds in which we live. As we open our hearts to serendipity and connection, we allow our love to flow freely as part of a natural, ever-moving circle of life. In flow, our love nurtures and grows the feelings of connectedness, comfort and belonging we seek. Our love rejuvenates ourselves, others and the environments in which we live. Love colours our lives with limitless joy and enchantment. The purity and positivity of loving energy can permeate all manner of borders and initiate all kinds of miracles. Comparing, competing and withholding have no place in love. Courage, clarity and a willingness to learn and grow are attitudes and qualities that support love to flourish within, around and between us all.

Sometimes we need assistance to learn the ways of love – to step beyond our shadows, hesitations, old ideas, and doubts, to dive deeply into life. To be both brave and vulnerable. To feel truly splendid and alive. Indeed, loving takes a willingness to embrace subtleties, transformations and challenges within and around us. Love asks us to surrender our disbelief, accept fresh energy to replenish our hearts, and embrace the power of daily miracles great and small. Love also teaches us openness to receiving limitless pleasure, comfort and inspiration in our lives as we learn to give and receive in gratitude.

There is so much to life – so much that we miss with our eyes, hearts and minds closed. As we open our hearts to love, loving and being loved, we learn and grow, transforming our lives for the better. We become richer, more sensitive and empathetic human beings, and our lived experiences of love help us to connect and share with others in meaningful, life-affirming ways. While at times we may be profoundly challenged by our lessons in love, we can allow love's powerful and enchanting gifts to eclipse our pain and revitalise our hearts.

Dear Heart

I am learning the ways of love each day.
Through every season of my life
I thank you for being with me —
my ever-faithful companion.

When things flow, life feels light.
When things become dense,
I can grow a little weary.

Each time I stumble or doubt myself
remind me that I can rely on you.
Help me to come back home to you,
so I need never feel alone.

May the love I give others
bring peace and joy.
May the love I give to myself
nourish me beyond all other loves.

As I venture on, teach me
to dive more deeply into my life.
Keep talking to me as I go, Heart,
helping me to know what I need to know
and see what I need to see.

May I be brave and passionate as I move forward,
and may I live with sensitivity and grace.

Thank you, Heart. Speak soon.

5. LOVE AND WELLBEING

Sufi mystic Rumi taught that if we wish to feel more alive, love is our truest health. Indeed, the experience of love — loving and being loved — strengthens our physical and emotional hearts, boosting our moods and immune systems. By supporting a positive, healthy environment in which all the cells in our body can thrive, the energy of love nourishes and elevates our complete wellbeing. Love is therapeutic, medicinal and transformative. It is the perfect remedy in almost every imaginable situation, and offers profound, heavenly support in the face of any kind of adversity. Where there is love there is life, and where there is life there is rich potential. When we truly connect with the healing, creative life force that love is, we cannot help but feel strengthened and inspired. Love is an antidote for pain and loneliness, fear and disconnection. By nature love nurtures our vitality, and in our experience of vitality, we may feel truly alive.

In his wonderful book *The Honeymoon Effect*, molecular biologist Bruce Lipton describes the biology of love, explaining why it is that in the process of 'falling in love' we feel so radiant and energised. Falling in love involves powerful biochemical processes that impact our thoughts, feelings and physiology. Indeed, the rich delights of feeling love help our hurries and worries to melt away, allowing us to relax and enjoy our lives with greater ease and pleasure. Love soothes tension, gives us strength, bolsters our self-esteem and nurtures our self-worth, imbuing us with greater confidence and peace.

With greater confidence and peace we may feel calmer and more balanced as we go about our lives. In love, especially the early stages of romantic love as described by Lipton with warmth and wit, our vision of things, especially our beloveds, becomes flavoured by the processes that our biological experiences of love set into motion. It is in this that the old adage 'love is blind' finds its meaning: the power of love can even cause our vision to suddenly become very selective!

Lipton goes on to explain how the tremendous wellness benefits of falling in love involve voluntary, self-started processes that, with intention, we can all learn to cultivate within and around us at any time. By doing so we can create lives rich in love and, thus, rich in wellness. In other words, by tuning into the energy and power of love, we can harness its miraculous benefits and transform ourselves on an epigenetic level. We needn't be in love with another person to experience this; we must quite simply live and be 'in love'. Epigenetics speaks to lifestyle factors within our very own control: factors we may harness to elevate our wellbeing and move beyond preconceived limitations presented by our genetic profiles and old stories. Our daily thoughts, feelings, words and actions shape our experience of wellness. With attention and care we can attune our thoughts, feelings, words and actions to love, creating internal and external environments supportive of our health and happiness.

The power of falling in love is by no means exclusive to romantic love. Loving what we do and doing what we love equally inspire our wellbeing. Bringing our passion, zest, initiative and creativity to life makes us more vital and inspired human beings. It is empowering to acknowledge that our lives are exactly what we make of them. Choosing to participate in hobbies, passions and interests that ignite our hearts brings meaning and excitement to our daily lives. Our love of our pursuits is expressive of our innermost desires and speaks to our uniqueness. We may enjoy climbing mountains, knitting jumpers, or making music. We may enjoy snuggling up with our loved ones or pets, writing letters, or learning new languages. Indeed, doing what we love and loving what we do allows us to be 'in love' each day, making the very best of each moment we have and nourishing our wellness.

Love's miraculous healing powers are riveting and are not to be underestimated. The love we feel for someone or something – a person, a pet, a project, a place – can breathe fresh air into our minds, hearts and spirits. The history of love is full of inspirational stories of miracles, triumphs, spontaneous healings and the tremendous power of grace. Our unfolding, daily experiences of love can reveal new levels of joy and peace we might previously have thought impossible for us, opening and replenishing our hearts.

To be loved and appreciated gives us the strength and support we need to evolve into more conscious, open-hearted and open-minded people – to follow our dreams and feel truly alive.

In love, we begin to experience ourselves as loveable people with precious gifts to offer. The experience of being loved nurtures our sense of self-esteem and self-worth, and, in harmony with our love and care for ourselves, fortifies us for life. In times of hardship, receiving love gives us the comfort, confidence and motivation we need to find and harness our innate courage. In all these ways and so many more, love empowers, delights and elevates us.

With a bigger-picture vision, we may explore the ways in which the energy of love has the power to heal the epidemics of fear, violence, loneliness and disconnection we face together. Observing the state of our collective wellness on earth, we might notice the hurried ways in which we live; the pressures under which we find ourselves; and the challenging relationships so many of us have with ourselves and each other. We can see these daily stresses degenerating our wellbeing on physical, mental and spiritual levels, thieving our health, comfort and joy.

Love is for everyone. We all need, deserve and yearn for love. We need to feel connected and thrive together in unison. In times gone by, banishment from our tribe was considered to be the ultimate punishment. To be banished from our community was to be disconnected from our wellspring of safety and vitality. Those banished would very often fall ill, even perish. Feeling a sense of belonging is just as vital for us today as it ever was. Being part of a community, a family or a group of people with a shared purpose nourishes our wellness and brings joy to our hearts.

Taking stock of such observations, we come to see a desperate, communal need for more kindness and compassion, patience and inclusivity on earth. Thankfully, love is a culmination of all these wonderful higher essences and virtues in action. Love brings immediate softening and healing to our own hearts and the hearts of others with whom we share our lives. By choosing compassionate, forgiving and peaceful pathways, each day we are all able to live lovingly, supporting our personal and collective wellbeing.

We can exercise, eat well and have carefully planned daily schedules designed to enhance our health and wellness. We can meditate, pray and philosophise about health and happiness. Yet, if we are disconnected from ourselves and each other, withholding of our love and unwilling to honour our passions and dreams, we will find it difficult to cultivate the depth of wellness and satisfaction we inherently know is available to us in this life. Cultivating true wellbeing by sowing seeds of love within and around us heals and transforms our lives. Let us learn the ways of love, allowing love to nourish, enrich and guide us forward.

Dear Heart

I am thankful for my wellbeing,
the energy I have for life.
For all the wonderful things I have done,
and all the wonderful things that await me.

May I honour and follow you so that my
energy for life stays vital and strong.

May I delight and nurture you,
give and receive love,
so that you may always feel refreshed
and very well looked after.

May I see that nourishing you
nurtures my body and mind
and that when you feel joy,
my spirit is ignited.

Help me to choose peaceful and joyous pathways
in loving support of my wellbeing.

Help me to see, know and care for myself
as the worthy and loveable person that I am.

May I treasure my uniqueness.
May I savour the beauty and mystery of my life.
May I live each day with passion,
and welcome you to guide me on.

Thank you, Heart.
Speak soon.

6. LOVE AND SELF-CARE

To love ourselves is a lifelong gift and precious art deserving of our devotion, time and care. When we love ourselves sincerely, wholeheartedly and unconditionally — something we can all learn to do — we transform our wellbeing and the wellness of all those whose lives we touch with our presence. Living by loving example, cultivating a kind, compassionate and authentic relationship with ourselves, we naturally encourage others to see the possibility of doing so too. In this way, self-love is not selfish; it is a profound part of our collective wellbeing. When we love and respect ourselves just as we are while working towards our dreams, we blossom.

Loving ourselves has nothing to do with ego, vanity and pride. To truly love ourselves is a natural and powerful choice we can all make in support of our personal growth, inner calm, and vital energy for life. Loving self-care involves suspending constant judgement of ourselves, making peace and joy with our inner voice, nurturing ourselves by spending time at home within, and expressing our authentic selves. Self-care involves loving life and trusting life to love us back, allowing divine grace to meet and support us at every turn as we bring our best to life each day. Indeed, when we do our very best, we can trust that life will do the rest.

Self-care involves committing to kind, clear and loving thoughts, and aligning our actions with our heart's desires. The love we give ourselves sets the tone for all other love in our lives. We are often on the hunt for love outside ourselves – be that validation, recognition, attention or approval in romantic love, friendships or professional relationships we build with others. It is impossible to receive exactly what we are looking for in the way of love, however, until we are able to grant that exquisite quality of real love unto ourselves, first and foremost. In the wise and beautiful words of writer and philosopher Helen Keller, what we are looking for isn't out there, it is within us. The gaps we feel in our emotional and spiritual lives are invariably spaces into which our own true love must pour and nestle, soothing, settling and fortifying us for life.

Our very own love is a powerful, personalised healing elixir tailor-made by – and just for – us. Drinking from our inner wellspring of love, we learn to thrive by gifting ourselves our own time, attention and care. We come alive in our own love. Nourished by our own love, we find our frequency elevated, our energy levels revitalised and our hearts replenished. In such an uplifted, expansive and vital state, it is hardly surprising that we welcome more loving people, moments and experiences into our days, as if by way of divine magnetism. With such riches on constant offer to us, we are wise to abandon any of our outworn, self-limiting habit patterns and beliefs in favour of practising loving self-care instead. This is not complicated philosophy. Indeed, like all the very best things in life, it is remarkably and gorgeously simple.

The concept that we are our own worst critics is bandied about but holding this belief is to our collective detriment. It is a notion supported, both wittingly and unwittingly, by our routinely unloving behaviours. In truth, we needn't be our own worst critics. In an ideal world – the kind of world we are striving to create together – each one of us would be our own greatest and most faithful support person. We would also be sincere and passionate in our support of one another.

Self-deprecation should not be confused with humility, especially when it results in us hiding our important and unique lights under proverbial bushels. The ways in which we judge and berate ourselves can be so unkind and unloving, when we wouldn't dream of treating others with such damaging thoughts and ideas. Intercepting unhelpful self-talk at the thought level is critical emotional intelligence. Learning to interrupt, question and rework our redundant thought processes means we may avoid the unhelpful words and acts that follow them. Cultivating and nurturing loving thoughts and a compassionate, supportive inner voice positively transforms our lives, even beyond recognition.

If we wish to experience more love, this is always and forever our place to begin – with our own thoughts, the very thoughts that create our worlds. We experience things as we choose to see them. As our thoughts change, the way we see things changes. As the way we see things changes, everything in our lives changes. Choosing to think, see and act with love is always our choice to make.

Beyond loving maintenance of our thoughts and self-talk – our daily foundations – we can incorporate various self-care rituals into our daily lives for sustaining nourishment. Self-care will look different to each and every one of us: from quiet nights and gentle walks in nature to lighthearted movies or evenings spent dancing.

Enjoying a practice of prayer, meditation or quietness can infuse our daily lives with greater peace and clarity. Routinely savouring slow stretches or quiet, soothing music can free and loosen our minds and bodies as we lead our daily lives. Drinking tea from a favourite cup can bring us comfort, as can reciting a heartfelt affirmation to fortify and uplift us. Our self-care rituals needn't be grandiose or complicated. Indeed, keeping things simple brings us joy. Making time for pleasure revitalises and fulfils us. We might love travelling, reading, baking cakes, or playing musical instruments. As we care for ourselves more lovingly each day, prioritising our bliss and joy becomes our way of life. When we are nourished, we may go forward to nourish others with whom we share our lives.

The all-knowing, all-sensing power of love meets us in the middle each time we consciously move towards it, acknowledging our efforts and replenishing our hearts with fresh optimism, vitality and faith. Love touches us and all things. We are never alone. Indeed, heavenly forces embrace and carry us in every moment. As we explore the more mysterious and invisible parts of love, we come to see ourselves as part of a bigger picture in which we timelessly and effortlessly belong. Woven into a resplendent fabric of life, our hearts form part of a perfect network offering us endless inspiration and a sense of belonging. In loving ourselves tenderly, we harmonise with greater love to create joyous lives we can truly celebrate and adore.

Dear Heart

I am learning to love myself
a little more each day.

When I am tender and patient with myself,
I know you are guiding me.

Love is for everyone, including me.
My love is for everyone, including myself.
Help me to love myself deeply and honestly,
and feel nourished by my very own time and care.

The more love I show myself,
the stronger and more peaceful I feel.
From a place of strength and peace,
I can be all I can and wish to be.

Heart, please help me to let go
of any outworn ideas I have held on to
about myself and my life.
I am ready to move forward now,
and I see new possibilities for myself.

May I make quiet moments to listen to you
so that I may hear what you have to say.

May I make time to honour you
and let your endless energy
imbue me with wisdom and joy.

7. LOVE AND BEING BUSY

In our fast-moving modern world, we can become 'too busy' to love and care for ourselves and each other tenderly. Running from A to B, ticking off our to-do lists, and meeting all the needs of the day, we can inadvertently neglect our relationships with ourselves and others. Nurturing loving relationships is essential for our health and happiness. We suffer when we allow ourselves to become too busy to take care of what really matters in our lives.

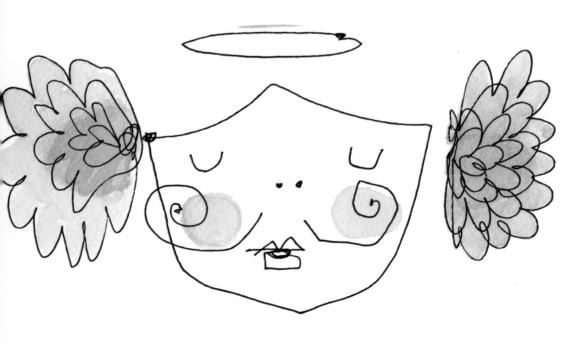

Being busy is a wonderful and legitimate excuse for a great variety of things in today's world. We all seem to be juggling and balancing so many activities and commitments each day that being overwhelmed, stressed, hurried and distracted are perfectly normal, acceptable states of being. So much so that in moments of spaciousness or reprieve we might feel unable to relax, and even chastise ourselves for being unproductive. Feeling overwhelmed or guilty when we slow down at last is a reality for so many of us. We tend to move rapidly, often too fast to fully see, feel, grow and embrace love. Love takes time, and love requires our attention – our presence. Being present here and now with ourselves and others is completely essential to cultivating meaningful and enduring relationships grounded in the power and grace of love. Slowing down enough to see, feel and appreciate love is essential for our wellbeing.

So many relationships – romantic and otherwise – come to an end due to neglect. Learning to meet emotional, physical and spiritual needs in our relationships is one of the greatest learnings and gifts in this life. Relationships take time and care, and if we are too busy – jam-packed and distracted in our daily lives – we miss critical signs that flag room for transformation and improvement in our bonds with ourselves and each other.

Making time for meaningful conversations, listening carefully, asking thoughtful questions, and letting our loved ones know they are treasured are examples of loving care in action. Poet Ralph Waldo Emerson wrote that we can never do a kindness too soon, for we never know how soon it will be too late. Indeed, when we awaken to the bittersweet impermanence of all things we realise that we must love ourselves and one another right now, not tomorrow or at some time to come, but right now – in the present – the only moment we truly have. The past is gone and the future is not here, nor is it guaranteed. We must make time and space for love now.

To have a friend is to be one. In our friendships and romances alike, we must show up and actively contribute to the health and happiness of our interpersonal connections. As with any kind of effort made in this life, we cannot expect to put in minimal time and care yet receive maximum satisfaction and enchantment. True romance is cultivated in a climate of unhurried comfort and bliss. With time and care, romantic love can provide a safe haven for lovers to find peace and joy in one another – to savour quiet moments of connection, profound empathy, mutual support and deep understanding. Similarly, poet Samuel Taylor Coleridge wrote that friendship is like a sheltering tree. With attention and nurturing, our friendships can become wonderful, uplifting retreats for our spirits – bonds in which our hearts are delighted and replenished.

Sometimes we get so busy that we stop doing, or forget to do, the things that we love. We disconnect from activities and passions that bring us joy, getting stuck in repetitive routines at the great expense of our health and happiness. We can get in the habit of putting our passions off as if we have all the time in the world, or as if pursuing our hobbies and interests needn't be a priority in our lives. We can allow ourselves to become so busy that in moments of free time, we have no energy left with which to explore our interests and desires. Rather, all we wish to do is retire our senses and, in passive ways, seek to be entertained.

Following our passions and hobbies is not a matter of indulgence, it is an essential commitment to nurturing our wellbeing. Exploring our creativity and really enjoying our lives brings us feelings of satisfaction and pleasure that make us more exciting and balanced human beings. When we take time to have fun, we become much more fun to be around. Others sense the positive energy of our inner fulfilment and enjoy the buoyancy we bring to life.

Moreover, the happy experiences we enjoy when pursuing our passions gift us with interesting things to talk about and share in daily life. Making time to do what we love and love what we do is not something to pursue in the future. It is a matter of daily practice to meet our very real needs for pleasure, peace and play. To love our lives doing wonderful things with care, be they even very simple or little things, is to live our lives to the fullest.

I always recommend taking up a passion that involves using one's hands. When we use our hands – be that by sewing, playing piano, making mosaics, building things or arranging flowers, any such lovely pursuit – we connect with our creative power. Our hands are so wonderful and so full of potential. As we use our hands in creative ways, we find ourselves dropping down from our busy, thinking heads into our feeling hearts. We begin to practise a kind of mindfulness in motion, feeling more relaxed and inspired as we go. If we wish to feel more love within and around us, we must quite simply enjoy things that make our hearts sing. In doing so, we replenish ourselves with love.

Time is what we make of it. With a scarcity mindset around time, we will never have enough. In contrast, if we believe that we have all the time we could ever need, we will always have enough. Making the very best of our lives means letting love guide our agendas for ultimate health and happiness. Reframing our connection to love – seeing that we can do all things with love, and lovingly – opens up new possibilities for each and every one of us. As we live our lives lovingly moment to moment, we naturally nurture ourselves and those with whom we share our worlds. Quality time and care for our relationships and passions needn't necessarily be sectioned off and diarised; it simply becomes who we are and what we do. Loving becomes our way of being. Living this way, we nourish our hearts and, as if by some kind of magic, find ourselves with more time and energy for ourselves, others and our various passions.

Dear Heart

Sometimes I feel too busy
to talk to you.
I can get very hurried
and forget to check in.

The thing I notice with gratitude
is that you don't seem to mind.
You are always there for me;
all I need to do is say hello.

In your constant example of love
I see I have so much to learn.
I am very humbled.

Please help me to make time
for the things that matter most in my life.
For the people and places I love,
and for my passions and dreams.

As I move forward,
help me to work together with time,
ensuring that time feels generous,
and that time is always enough for me.

May I learn to relish living slowly,
noticing the beauty of small things,
and taking ample rest to replenish you.

As I talk to you now,
help me to be still for a moment.
As I breathe in and out,
let me come back home to love.

8. LOVE AND COURAGE

Love gives and takes enormous courage, and courage gives and takes great faith. When fear suggests we can't, love responds: 'Try, perhaps you can ...' When disappointment demoralises us, love responds with patience and perseverance. When heartbreak says we may never love again, love answers: 'Just you wait and see.' When hurts and judgements suggest our hearts aren't safe, love asks for our trust again and again. The stories of rich and meaningful lives lived to the fullest will always show us that it is better to endeavour than not to try at all. To soar with passion and determination and fall, than never to fly. To open our hearts, even in the face of fear, than to lock away our love. Indeed, splendid and courageous lives are led by love.

Love, such a natural thing, can come about very organically. It can happen and grow easily, always magically, sometimes without us even realising. People can come into our lives and become friends quite effortlessly. American novelist and poet Ray Bradbury described the formation of friendship like the filling of a vessel with various kindnesses, drop by drop. As drops of kindness fill our vessels to overflowing in friendship, so too do our hearts run over with love. The idea that friendships and romances can form in this natural way – as a result of a series of exchanges that endear and entrust ourselves to each other – is a beautiful notion.

At other times, precise initiative is warranted to instigate and form new relationships. These acts or moments of reaching out take a beautiful mix of vulnerability and courage. What if our feelings and expressions of affection in love or friendship are unrequited? What if we were to extend our love or friendship in good faith and feel rejected? In friendship, as in romance, we put our hearts on the line when we offer our love to others. We expose ourselves to hurt, loss, humiliation, rejection

… all the very things we fear. And yet, we also expose ourselves to the possibility of experiencing the deepest delight in love: the most profound connections, and the most unforgettably beautiful, life-changing experiences imaginable. Without endeavouring in love, our lives are left unlived. Our innermost hopes and dreams go unexplored, and our heart's desires fade, unfulfilled. Cultivating the courage to listen to and follow our hearts in daily life, we really can make our dreams of love come true.

We may never know quite how things could have eventuated had we had the courage to have acted and expressed ourselves differently in certain moments past; had we had greater faith in ourselves, life and love then. While regretting past inactions or shortcomings would be a waste of our precious energy, nurturing the courage to choose love now quite simply opens us up to the richness of giving and receiving in this moment and all moments to come. Choosing love reveals to us the true power and beauty of living: the joy and inspiration of meaningful bonds with others, and the divine satisfaction of leading heart-centred lives.

Choosing love now means speaking our hearts and minds bravely, honesty and carefully, expressing our care for ourselves and others and living in a spirit of gratitude for life itself.

Courage in love also sees us diving into new things outside of our comfort zone with a healthy sense of curiosity and adventure. Our love extends beyond our relationships with ourselves and others and weaves its way into all things, pastimes and pleasures that make our hearts sing. Exploring new activities, embarking on new adventures and nurturing hobbies and passions in our daily lives fulfils our innate human need for creative play. Creative play keeps us youthful, inspired, light and engaged. Creative play and pleasure help us to grow our courage and confidence, both independently and within communities of like-spirited people. Taking a joyous leap of faith into a new endeavour can truly replenish our hearts.

It also takes courage to love in the face of unloving behaviour — when we experience unkindness or conflict, or when loving doesn't feel easy. In such moments, while it may be tempting to be unkind, argumentative or unloving in return, we are always wise to remember the powerful aphorism, 'An eye for an eye and the whole world is blind'. When we become the change we wish to see in the world, we see no place for unloving behaviour.

We simply find peaceful ways to move forward without fuss, pain, hurt or holding on. In doing so, we gift and surprise those with whom we share our lives, planting healing seeds of peace that blossom within and around us, growing more love.

We never know quite how far the little seeds of our love will travel and fruit beyond our own lives, though we may delight in the mysterious and wonderful ways our love will touch, move and inspire others.

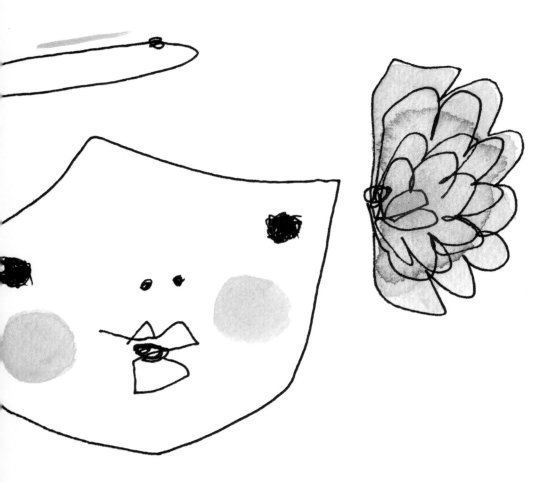

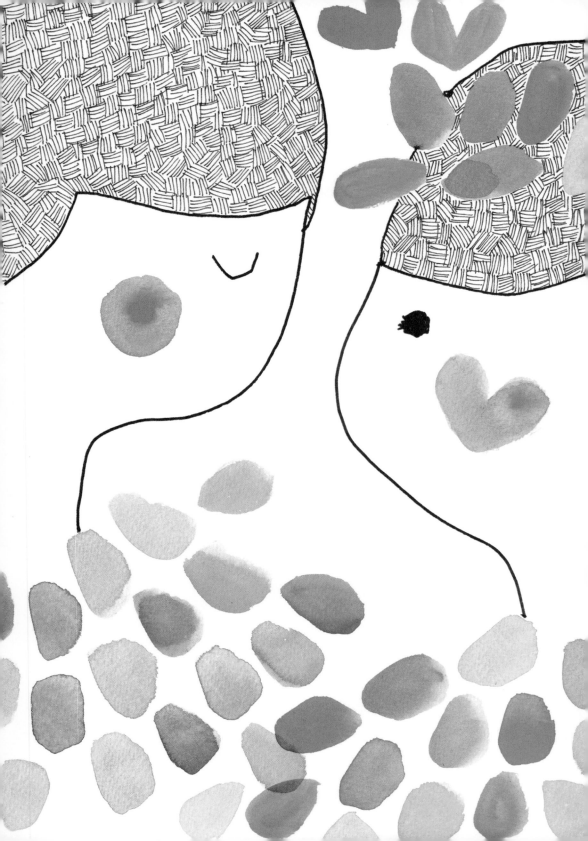

When chapters in our lives close – profound chapters in our relationships with others, chapters in our career paths, or even in our relationships with ourselves – it takes enormous courage to know when to let go. To let go in faith that life will go on, and to trust that we and those we love will be held and remain safe through life's inevitable shifts and changes. We must cultivate the courage to see and acknowledge things as they are, without forcing them to be another way. We must lovingly recognise and honour what is most natural for us, most supportive of our wellbeing, as this is essential self-care. In our relationships with ourselves, just as in our relationships with others, it is powerful to recognise when we have grown beyond outworn patterns, circumstances or behaviours that deplete and inhibit us. With awareness and courage, we can release unloving thoughts, situations and ways gracefully, even if they have become very comfortable or familiar to us. Every time we take courageous steps forward in the way of wellness and peace, we replenish our hearts and let love grow.

How do we cultivate courage? By growing our resilience. Growing our resilience means developing a kinder, more encouraging inner voice that supports and inspires us at every turn. This inner voice comforts and fortifies us in the face of our perceived 'failures' – disappointment when things don't go the way we thought they 'should' or would – and our perceived 'imperfections' – illusions that we, what we do or how we do it are somehow 'not enough' or 'not good enough'. A kinder inner voice strengthens us in the face of judgement and self-judgement. We often harbour unrealistic expectations that we 'should' be very good at something the first time we attempt it, chastising ourselves when we simply need more time to learn and grow. We may also allow ourselves to be inhibited – even let go of our dreams – due to our own or others' criticism, negative feedback or disapproval. We must return to ourselves with loving conviction in such moments, and this is made possible by practising and feeling great faith in ourselves. Michelangelo regarded faith in ourselves as 'our best and safest course'. As we nurture more love within and around us, we naturally become more resilient and self-assured. With loving self-respect and self-approval, we create peace and safety for ourselves. We can then move about our lives feeling strong and free.

We also grow our resilience by nurturing our faith in life. Growing our faith in life involves trusting in things we may not be able to see, nor understand. Courageous belief in life and love can take great leaps of faith. Agape – universal love – refers to a great love for all life and creation. Realising that our lives are governed and connected by tremendous loving energy within and around us, and learning to gracefully surrender to this truth with awareness that we are held and that we belong, is life changing. When we are attuned to universal love, we begin to see and experience ourselves and life very differently: like drops of water in an ocean moving together with all other drops – unique but together, interdependent, endless and always connected. Cultivating the courage to listen to our hearts and move in a greater sea of love, we become part of building a happier, healthier, more wonderful world.

Dear Heart

In the story of my life
I have had to be very brave.

Thank you for gifting me the courage
to move forward,
even when I have not been able
to see my next steps ahead.

Please strengthen my faith
at difficult times,
and help me to trust
in the sacred design of my life.

Thank you for your endless support
as I learn to see and know myself with love.
Help me to speak to myself kindly,
and show myself the care I deserve.

Thank you for the courage
to dive into life and new things.

May I be curious and adventurous.
May I truly appreciate my life.

Courage is asked of me each day.
At any moment I waver,
let me feel your loving presence,
and fill me with all the strength I could ever need.

Help me to live bravely, richly and deeply, Heart.
Show me how to savour
and to love all there is to life.

9. LOVE AND COMFORT

In the comfort of love, we find great solace. Above and beyond the tenderness and care we can all give and receive — a holding hand, a quiet embrace, little messages of care to let us know that we are being thought of — we are all eternally embraced by the warmth and light of an endless, greater love that dwells ever presently within and around us. With our acknowledgement of this great love, we become the recipients of deep and endless comfort.

Italian philosopher Leo Buscaglia wrote that we are wise never to underestimate the power of a kind word, a smile, an honest compliment or the smallest act of caring, as, unbeknownst to us, our love could turn a life around. In the sharing of our love, we can be far more influential and comforting than we may ever know. Taking time to listen carefully to each other, to become more attuned to our own thoughts and feelings and those of others with whom we live, helps us to better support one another with love. A word of encouragement in a moment of doubt can change the course of our path. The touch of our hands can speak volumes when our words might fall short. A tight embrace can strengthen us and make us feel safe when we feel vulnerable, enabling us to move forward with fresh courage. Love is comfort.

Mindful awareness of ourselves, each other and life helps us to sense when a tender word could be spoken or a gesture of support, affection or acknowledgement be made at just the right time. When we awaken to the present moment and live our lives right here and now, we notice that each moment is the perfect moment for love. We see that each conversation – each experience – can be touched and made all the more meaningful and magical with our love. Indeed, we can bring a rounded sense of peace and comfort to all that we do in our everyday lives, just by choosing to live lovingly. To live lovingly is to think, speak and act with thoughtfulness and care. Living lovingly we begin to feel more at home within ourselves and within the world at large than ever before. We learn to create and dwell in peace.

While comfort in love has many different faces, the calm, grounding essence of safety that love brings touches us with the same peaceful kiss. The love between a parent and child can provide protection and assuredness at the door of a big world. Intimate love in romantic relationships can create safe havens for lovers to nestle into and, at the end of a long day, offer the bliss of homecoming into each other's arms. Love in friendships, like a sheltering tree, creates space for open-heartedness and the sharing of life's ebbs and flows. Life is better shared, and in our relationships with each other, we find portals to all kinds of love. As we explore each new avenue of life, we can choose love as our constant companion.

We are the best givers of comfort. The most powerful comfort we could ever receive is that which we grant to, and nurture within, ourselves. We often unwittingly scare ourselves with frightful, negative thoughts that worry and unsettle us. Yet we always have a choice to cultivate a gentler, kinder inner language with our conscious attention, time and care. When we find ourselves thinking unhelpful or stressful thoughts we can quite simply notice and interrupt them. We can ask any uncomfortable thought a question or two, and, in doing so, test its boundaries. Is this right and true? Is this helpful? With these questions we can come back to centre, transforming our thought process in that very moment. We can then opt for a more comforting thought to settle ourselves and allow us to feel safe and sound again. I love you or I am here for you, we might hear ourselves say. We can even ask our hearts to help us find the most nourishing thought possible in place of our old thought, and assist us on our way. We are never alone. At the end of any little prayer is the greater, all-knowing love of which we are naturally a part, for which we naturally yearn and in which we deserve to live.

Beyond the peace and joy we can grow with our gentler thoughts and words, thoughtful acts of loving care can provide us with immense comfort. Tender, kind gestures we can extend to ourselves and those we love needn't be complicated to feel very decadent and rejuvenating.

A phone call, a love letter or a helping hand can turn the tide of a weary heart. We might slow down to enjoy a quiet cup of tea in a stressful moment, or run a warm scented bath to nurture an aching body. We might take some quiet time to breathe, rest, meditate or pray. Taking ourselves or our loved ones for a special little outing such as a walk or a lovely morning tea can soothe, inspire, and restore our energy. Spending time in nature can bring us immense solace too, as it is in nature that we truly come home. The warmth of the sun, the song of the waves, dappled light through dancing leaves – the beauty of nature works with us and upon us as we recalibrate and nurture our hearts. The unconditionally loving company of our pets can also bring us immense comfort when our spirits need a little lift. The loyalty and devotion we receive from our wonderful animal companions can imbue us with such joy, comfort and delight.

Feeling the warmth and security of true comfort matters to us as human beings because it helps to fortify and replenish our hearts. When we are safe and comfortable, we feel peaceful. When we feel peaceful, we can put our personal energy to great use, experiencing more bliss in daily life and offering our loving care to others. When we allow love to move through us, we always have enough love to give and share. Comforting others needn't take from our energy and deplete us – rather, it can grow and nurture the energy of love we feel within and around us. Sufi mystic Rumi wrote never to give from our deepest well but rather to give from our overflow. Giving love in this way, the joy and comfort that bubbles over from within us as we take loving care of ourselves can bring peace and comfort to all those with whom we share our lives. Herein lies the awe-inspiring power and beauty of comfort in love.

Dear Heart

At the beginning and end of each day
and indeed at any moment I please,
let me place my hand upon you
and return home within.

May the comfort of your endless love
give me courage and inspiration.

At any time I need strength
may my gentle, loving attention replenish you.
May I always find ways to nurture myself,
and let myself feel the peace of love.

Heart, as I learn to take care of you,
my life becomes so much more graceful.
As I learn to find comfort within me,
the world around me echoes my joy.

May the love I have to give
bring comfort to others,
and may my own warmth and care
grow more peace on earth.

10. LOVE AND COMPASSION

Compassion is an essential part of love, as feeling compassion allows us to step beyond our own feelings so that we may actively relate to, and feel with, others. The definition of compassion is to suffer with one another. While suffering is quite a dense word, it is used in Zen Buddhism to describe any sensation, thought process or circumstance that draws us away from peace — away from ourselves and from love. Considering suffering in this way, we see that navigating the natural ups and downs of daily life involves an awareness of our own and others' suffering and a willingness to alleviate as much of it as we possibly can through conscious, mindful living. With empathy, sensitivity and tenderness, we may support ourselves and each other to move through life with greater ease, joy and peace. This is compassion.

Jane Austen wrote that there is no charm equal to tenderness of heart. Indeed, tenderness is a beautiful human quality that connects, nurtures and fortifies us on our paths of life. We can all recognise how nourishing it is to feel the loving support and care of those with whom we share our lives; to feel understood by others who take the time to care for us and acknowledge our thoughts and feelings. The love we may grow and share with one another through our compassion demonstrates the strength of softness and the softness of strength.

All meaningful, respectful and loving relationships are built upon a foundation of compassion – a desire to understand ourselves and one another, and a genuine willingness to offer our support whenever we can. Intuiting when others may need a little extra tenderness and care, as we ourselves need at times, is compassion in action.

With our empathy and sensitivity, we may be proactive in love. Noticing if someone is feeling left out, shaky on their feet, lost for words or close to tears, we may move in to offer a touch of support, a soothing word, or some gesture of encouragement, however small, to help transform any given moment with our love.

When we notice ourselves and others feeling overwhelmed, sad or weary, we might see an opportunity for tenderness rather than a motivational push along. You can do it! and Stay strong! have their rightful time and place, as do the compassionate words, I am here for you, I understand or take your time.

Moments in which compassion may be extremely powerful are moments in which we choose not to be hurried on, nor to brush our feelings away and keep our chins up. Rather, moments in which gentle love will speak to and renew our hearts.

In understanding and respecting ourselves, we may better understand and respect others. The more self-aware and attuned we are to our own idiosyncrasies, thoughts and feelings, the more understanding and aware we may be to those of others. Such insight inspires greater patience, kindness and tolerance, as, like a mirror, compassion helps us to see ourselves in others and others in us. We notice our commonalities, shared fears, suffering and struggles. With this insight, rather than being judgemental or impatient, we can dig deeper to draw on a greater love to connect us and replenish our hearts. We can transform our impatience, judgement and unkindness into love through compassion, and nurture our collective peace and wellness.

As we grow more compassionate towards ourselves and each other, we become more sensitive, tender and empathetic human beings. We grow stronger, wiser and more loving, and come to enjoy richer, more fulfilling lives. A caveat for highly sensitive people – empaths who by nature feel others' feelings as if they were their own – is that compassion can be cultivated and gifted without it having to be felt at our own expense. When we learn to give from the overflow of our love, as poet and mystic Rumi teaches us to do, we keep the deepest waters in our wells of love for ourselves by necessity. In other words, we can ensure that when we give our loving energy to others, we reserve ample love, time and care especially for ourselves in order to thrive in our own lives.

Buddha taught that if our compassion excludes ourselves, it is incomplete. Our self-compassion is the very basis for the compassion we can gift to others. We can be compassionate and empathetic people, sensitive to the suffering of others, without denying ourselves the pleasure and joy of our own inner lives and feelings, nor compromising our wellbeing, mind, body or spirit. Indeed, we can relate to others in tenderness and truth while restoring our own energy for life. This just takes a little self-awareness and – for empaths in particular – healthy boundaries and ample, loving self-care. For more on self-care, please turn to pages 64–73.

In the face of the immense suffering we see on earth – that of human beings, animals and our planet all included – it is very understandable that we may often feel overcome, sometimes even helpless. Compassion offers us a proactive way to circulate love within and around us – to grow more love on earth and, in doing so, empower us to change the world. Compassionate love starts with and within us, then extends to the various creatures and environments that bring shape and meaning to our daily lives. Over time compassionate love, by virtue of its tremendous ripple effect, reaches out in broader ways, creating little miracles we may never quite know about, but that help lighten life on earth all the same. The more deeply we explore compassion, the more we may understand it as a truly dynamic, healing and empowering way of love. With our compassionate thoughts, words and actions, we can say and do so much.

Feeling understood, seen and heard replenishes our hearts, as does understanding, seeing and hearing others with whom we share life. We naturally feel calmer, happier and more resilient when we feel loved, respected and looked after, and in our care for others we can experience bliss and fulfilment too. We can always offer the gift of our love – the most beautiful gift we have to give – through our compassion. Taking the time to support one another in delicate, thoughtful and sensitive ways encourages our hearts to feel safe so they may express themselves freely, connect with other hearts, and blossom.

Dear Heart

As I awaken to love,
help me to cultivate compassion
so that I may be tender and kind
towards myself and others.

May choosing compassion
bring meaning and comfort
to myself and others
each day of my life.

May listening to you
and exploring possibilities
for collective peace through love
imbue me with a true sense of purpose.

Help me to see that loving kindness,
especially when it takes great strength and faith,
supports deep healing in my own life
and in the lives of all those I love.

May I be filled with joy and inspiration,
the desire to love and understand,
the grace of patience,
and the passion to create positive change.

11. LOVE AND LOSS

In love's mysterious and profound splendour, we are fortified and vulnerable in equal measure. Taoist philosopher Lao Tzu wrote that being loved by someone deeply gives us strength, while loving someone deeply gives us courage. Loss is a part of love. And if the amount that we love is proportionate to the amount we grieve, those of us who love deeply will feel tremendous heartache in the face of loss. Grief comes hand in hand with our courage to love. While the experience of grief may be unthinkable, immeasurable and at times feel utterly insurmountable, we are wise to draw encouragement and comfort from the words of the poet Alfred, Lord Tennyson: "Tis better to have loved and lost than never to have loved at all.' Our hearts call us to be brave, as to shy away from love for fear of loss is to shy away from life.

Life asks us to be courageous in love, time and time again. This can be terribly challenging when, in the face of loss, our hearts can feel very weary. Simple things we once found easy to manage can become difficult, even overwhelming. Sadness might cause us to feel lacklustre, unenthused and absent. We might notice that our confidence and joy feel diminished, and that we need much more rest to replenish our hearts, minds and bodies. Tending to ourselves with loving respect during these times is the ultimate way to honour our feelings and sow new seeds of love. These little seeds begin within us, be they very small, and, over time, grow.

Bolstering our hearts in daily life allows us to feel more present and resilient in the face of immense challenges such as the loss of a loved one, or the end of a significant relationship. Such life-altering challenges can bring great feelings of sadness, loneliness, fatigue and disconnection. Caring for our hearts takes time and devotion. Replenishing our hearts at thought level means choosing thoughts to comfort and uplift us, even intercepting and upgrading difficult and uneasy thoughts as they arise, helping us to find our feet. The words we speak and actions we take to nurture a loving, honest and compassionate relationship with ourselves and others enable us to build meaningful connections and true inner peace. In a spirit of self-care and kindness, we are able to grow and readily access deep reservoirs of energy and bravery within as we move forward, one step at a time. Taking time to nourish our hearts in daily life helps us to navigate the immensity of our feelings as they arise, and as we endeavour to make sense of the breathtaking impermanence of all things.

In the inevitability of loss, how can we be brave enough to love? We can begin powerfully, surrendering with gratitude and wonder to the infinite richness and beauty of life. In surrendering to life, we take the joyous and challenging parts, the rational and irrational parts, the laughter and tears, noisy and quiet times, the love and the grief. We may hold life in its simplicity and complexity all at once, choosing to be 'all in' and fully present. We can commit to life, appreciating the privilege it is to exist and to feel. We can choose to see that life is what we make of it, and feel inspired, understanding that a life well lived is a life well loved.

While the 'loss' of love might feel like disconnection or separation, and love might fool us by feigning some kind of permanence, perhaps solidity, in the form of a person, experience, dream or object of our profound affection, the essence and energy of love is boundless, timeless and far more magical than words may allow us to express. Writer and philosopher Helen Keller wrote that what is most precious cannot be seen or touched, but felt in the heart. No one can take our feelings from us, nor can any amount of

time or space diminish real love. Love is expansive and knows no bounds. It is the energy of life, of which we are all part. Enjoying the gifts we are given by virtue of our human connection and sensitivity, and by the grace of our natural inclination and potential to love, we may live rich and wonderful lives.

Living fully in the moment means that we may love bravely and completely. Acknowledging the uncertainty and impermanence of things, we can choose kindness over callousness and cultivate a greater, more potent sense of perspective. We can choose to speak from our hearts, not leaving precious things unsaid. We can choose to forgive, and never allow the sun to set on our petty squabbles. We may brave life with zest, not hiding our love under bushels – not manipulating, overthinking, or withholding our love. Living this way, love ultimately becomes us, and we become it.

Exploring and challenging our more rigid, material ways of seeing, suspending our limiting thoughts, and attuning ourselves to love's more subtle, mystical and enriching possibilities offers us immense insight and peace. Being aware of our brief human experience on earth in light of the free, eternal life of our spirits allows us to find meaning and perspective in our love and grief. Albert Einstein described the rational mind as a creative servant, and intuition as a gift. With a little practice, tuning into our hearts, we may use our intuitive gifts to sense and live beyond our material realm and amid great love: timeless and effortless love. The love of our dear ones and ancestors, past, present and future; the care of guardian angels; and the vital energy of life itself. In navigating loss, we may also wish to explore ideas of acceptance and open-heartedness. We may gently begin to draw on the support, understanding and tenderness of those with whom we share our lives. In our grief we may feel terribly isolated, and yet, so many others can relate to us.

Opening our hearts to the replenishment afforded by true connection, conversation and respect for our shared experience of life, we imbue ourselves with the peace and comfort for which we yearn. While sadness may push us internally, to be with ourselves, necessarily healing and restoring our hearts in the sanctuary of our inner world, there comes a time when we must choose to embrace love and life again. This is a matter of opening our hearts to the endless presence and power of love within and around us at all times, even, and especially, in our most difficult hours. This may involve saying yes to a cup of tea with a friend. Taking a walk in nature. Listening to some beautiful music. Opening the windows to welcome fresh air and sunlight. Doing something simple to bring us joy. Courageously and faithfully welcoming love again, we find fresh energy, solace and motivation. We begin to transform our grief into love again, and, in doing so, take part in the sacred and extraordinary circle of life.

Dear Heart

Talk to me in my darkest,
most difficult hours —
when I feel you hurting
and don't quite know what to do.

Keep talking to me
so that I may stay with you
and feel your presence.
Guide me, one breath at a time,
to sense the comfort of love within me.

Dear Heart, when I am so sad
and feel you breaking,
may I find ways to let light in
and replenish you.

May little inspirations come to me —
gentle thoughts or things I can do,
to bring myself peace and comfort.

In the magic and beauty
of the mystery of life,
help me to make peace
with change.

Show me silver linings,
reasons for joy
and endless serendipity
to refresh my faith in love.

12. TRANSFORMATIONAL LOVE

Choosing love takes just a moment, yet it can transform a day, even change an entire life. It is wonderful to explore the power of love, especially during times in which we must dig very deep to return to love. Love awaits us when we face our fears, when we try to make sense of injustice and unkindness, even when we struggle to forgive and move on. There is no moment in which love abandons us. With greater awareness of ourselves and others, we may make sense of love's potential and harness it to transform our moment-to-moment experience of life.

Let us take some time now to explore our ability to positively transform any moment or situation by choosing love. This is a life-changing art that begins with us, and cultivates peace and joy not only in our own hearts but in the hearts of all those with whom we share life.

Each day we may face
various challenges, injustices,
disappointments and unkindnesses.
Adding pain atop pain does not
grow love; it only compounds our
collective grief and loss. Challenging
as it may feel, we must have faith
in love's way to balance, make
sense and make right of things,
albeit in subtle, invisible ways over
greater time and space. Trusting
love wholeheartedly may warrant
the suspension of our disbelief, yet
we will soon find precious, vital
energy being freed by our constant
choosing of love, energising us to
go forward and make the changes
we wish to see. Positive, enduring
change is generated by love, not
by judgement, revenge or fear.
Mindfulness teacher Sri Chinmoy
wrote that if we wish to change
the world, we don't need to go out
to change it — we must rather go
out to love it. In loving our world,
our world is changed. In loving
ourselves and one another, we
are changed.

Living as feeling people among
other human beings with their own
hurts and hurries, fears and stresses,
is no easy feat — and yet, sharing
our lives is one of the richest, most
nourishing human experiences.

Noticing moments in which we feel compelled to react hastily, retaliate or seek revenge, for example, are powerful opportunities to explore the power of love. Approaching any exasperating situation with love, rather than berating ourselves for feeling our feelings, we may firstly observe how completely natural our feelings are. Our hearts can feel ruffled at times, and so be it. With self-compassion we may settle our hearts and ease our way forward.

Acknowledging our response to any situation with loving self-awareness, we may open our hearts to the others involved. We might like to observe that those being unkind or unjust towards us or others are feeling very angry or very hurt themselves. Acknowledging this might evoke our compassion for them. We too might be able to relate to acting out when feeling hurt, or to behaving in ways we thought were appropriate when we didn't know any better. At this point the light of love can illuminate our next steps forward. Perhaps we will feel gifted with a little more patience, empathy and understanding; maybe greater strength or clarity will land. Indeed, love graces us with timely gifts very naturally when we are anchored by it, and, over time, responding lovingly becomes organic, even joyously effortless for us.

Being discerning and cultivating thoughtful, agile responses with time and care is a wonderful part of living as conscious human beings. On the other hand, judging indiscriminately, being ignorant or flippant with our assertions and opinions, especially of others, can cause great division, hurt and unrest. Criticising, diminishing or excluding other people for their difference is lovelessness in action. We can be very intelligent people and yet find ourselves, albeit unwittingly, judging others in various ways – on face value, or by way of culture, gender, race or faith. In the cloudiness of such moments, love asks us to pause and see our shared humanity first and foremost: the things, feelings and experiences that connect us and bind us.

The transformative power of taking this loving pause is profound, as if offers us a chance to assess the truth of what we are thinking – to ask ourselves just how much we know and understand, and to actively choose love. In doing so, we allow empathy and compassion to challenge our views, opening up possibilities to learn and grow. How would it feel to be judged without being known in our completeness? Behind our actions, decisions, thoughts and beliefs there is always a story. A moment anchoring ourselves back into love opens up tremendous possibilities for connection, transformation and healing. The things that make us different are the things that make us unique and special. Choosing love means seeing each individual as a human being with a very unique story, yet woven from the same cloth as we are.

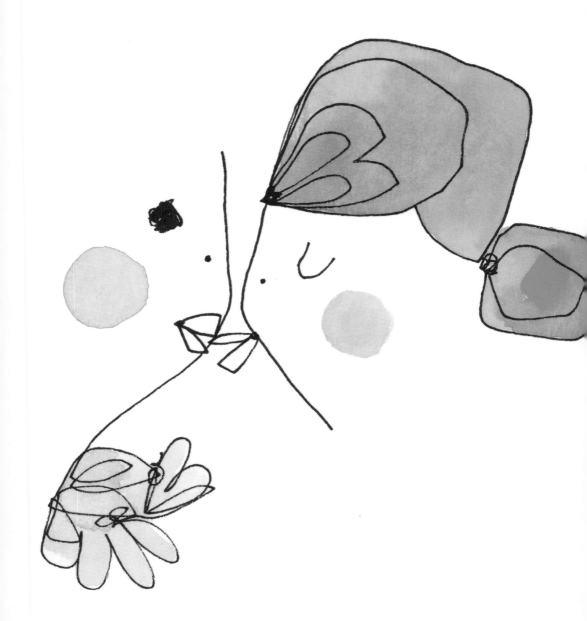

Observing the ways in which love can triumph over and transform fear is another fascinating and empowering exercise. Seeing our fears with love means noticing that our fears have a very specific purpose, and that they have invariably been there to protect us. Our fears are often signs of our love and care for ourselves. We want to keep ourselves safe and out of danger. We want to live our lives feeling happy and at peace. Observing our fears through the eyes of self-love and self-care helps us to transcend any damaging ideas about our fears being weaknesses. Indeed, the design of our thinking and feeling, while at times very easy to confuse, lament or misunderstand, is inherently intelligent, intuitive and self-preserving. Beneath our fear lies our love, be that love for ourselves, for others, or for life itself.

Fear of losing love means that we truly sense love in our lives – that we are living, breathing, sensing human beings, living the full richness of life's experience. Fear of illness or death expresses our value for life. Fear of being hurt reflects our self-respecting desire to know and feel the peace and joy we seek within ourselves and within our relationships. Fear of failure is often a reflection of our effort – that we have cared enough to do our very best. It warrants our loving attention that we were courageous enough to put ourselves into the field in the first place, to endeavour to do something with our time, effort and care. Fear of failure without endeavouring at all is a fear of losing face or feeling in some way inadequate. Through loving eyes, we can see that we are simply human beings that want to feel good enough. We want to be successful and to be loved in our lives, and this is perfectly natural. In these more self-compassionate ways, we can see the power of love to shine light and turn the tide on our various fears, allowing us to see ourselves and our lives in very new ways.

There is a good pinch of love in our fear, as there is a good pinch of fear in our love. Looking at the beautiful symbols for yin and yang, we can observe a poignant visual for the natural coexistence of these vital energies. When we love, we feel a sprinkling of fear for the loss of that love, just as underpinning our fear is the powerful energy of love and care. Love has much to do with safety. Beginning with us, the all-encompassing, unconditional energy of love can offer us the solace and comfort we seek in order to move forward in as much peace and joy as possible, even in a busy world brimming with highs, lows, and challenges of all kinds.

Refreshing our perspective through love helps us to replenish our hearts and transform self-limiting beliefs and behaviours that hold us back as we travel forward. Sufi mystic Rumi observed that we were born with wings, and questioned why we would choose to crawl through life. In love's limitless energy, we can all feel strengthened to aim higher, grow and flourish.

Dear Heart

As I awaken to the power of love,
I watch my life transform in wonderful ways.

Tuning in to your guidance each day,
I notice your timely insights with gratitude.
I am thankful for the prompts you give me
as I make my way forward in peace and joy.

I see myself with compassion
and my thoughts and feelings soften.
I treat myself with tenderness
and my days ease and lighten.

As I see others with care,
I know what love looks like.
As I treat others with kindness,
I feel you, replenished.

Heart, help me to feel safe at all times,
nestled into the comfort of my own love.
Help me to see that the world I create around me
reflects the world I nurture within me.

Each day as I let go
of that which I no longer need —
thoughts, things and old ideas —
may I feel uplifted by my freedom.

May I replenish you each day
with the respect you deserve,
taking the time and care
to live a life of love.

13. LOVE AND FORGIVENESS

Forgiveness is a tremendously important part of love. Forgiveness of ourselves and others frees us to live lives of peace, freshness and joy. Those we love can do and say hurtful things to us in haste and thoughtlessness, at times even cruelly with unkind intent. We too can say or do damaging things in moments of insensitivity or overwhelm, then realise soon after that we have let calamity and a loss of perspective get the better of our senses.

While hurtful behaviour may be the result of plain carelessness, most hurtful behaviour stems from unresolved hurt within ourselves. Alas, when we hurt ourselves and others we diminish ourselves all the more, compounding our despair. We often forget that by holding onto things – painful old memories or troublesome grudges – we hurt ourselves deeply. We may think we are teaching others a lesson by making them pay their dues, maintaining a ledger of rights and wrongs and keeping score, yet all the while our unforgiving ways burden us most of all.

The hurt of unforgiveness is held in our mind-body, where it creates stress and pain. Left unrecognised and unattended, this stress and pain plays out in our emotional landscapes and physical bodies. Our unforgiveness can make us stiff and inflexible, restless and unkind. It can cause blockages within the flow of our bodily functions, and dull the environment we create for our cells to exist and, ideally, thrive in. All the while, forgiveness is always an option, and one that, with a little practice, can more easily come to mind and heart over time.

Choosing to see ourselves with deep compassion, we cultivate the peace and courage to see and explore things as they are. We find ourselves better able to integrate emotions and events as they happen, and we strengthen our wellbeing. Unburdening ourselves of any unnecessary excess baggage, we feel so much lighter. In the freedom of our lightness, we can find the inspiration and strength to extend the same respect and grace of forgiveness to others in our lives. Living this way, we circumvent a great amount of unnecessary suffering.

When we refuse to forgive ourselves for our own shortcomings, mistakes and perceived failures, we inevitably find it very difficult to forgive others too. Forgiveness begins deep within ourselves, in a spirit of unconditional love.

A heart refreshed by perpetual forgiveness does not hold on to things without need. Rather, it busies itself with the beauty of life and higher pursuits of passion, creativity and love.

When we see that the patchwork of love is woven with profound lessons, lessons we cannot learn without traversing all manner of topography in all kinds of conditions, we see that the challenging terrain of love, including practising forgiveness, is quite possibly the richest ground there is. Once we learn to forgive, a new way of being opens up to us; walking through this open door, we experience the embrace of peace and comfort that we, by nature, yearn to know.

It is well understood that we hurt the ones we love the most: those with whom we share our lives most intimately. Love can cause us to act in strange, even confusing ways, and sometimes we are the ones who require others' forgiveness. While bolstering our sense of happiness and self-esteem, love can also make us vulnerable. For some, this vulnerability will emerge as jealousy, bitterness and unreasonable behaviour. Paradoxically, this debilitating behaviour is born of the same seed of love: our need to be seen, to be safe and to be adored.

Many deep rifts result from basic misunderstandings – misunderstandings that could be quite simply resolved through clear communication, bravery and open-heartedness. Over time, a simple disconnection in communication can morph beyond all sense and reason, taking on a life of its own.

While we may truly love one another, we may not always comprehend each other, nor know the words or ways in which to truly express ourselves. We may not know how to ask for or offer forgiveness; how to say sorry or let things go. Overcome by our thoughts and feelings, we can lose our perspective, failing to see and understand the situations in which we find ourselves.

Important words or sentiments can be lost in anxious or steely silence, or in hasty, careless exchanges. Learning forgiving words and ways takes a willingness to love, to see and experience ourselves and each other in peace. While challenging at first, forgiving swiftly allows us to experience swift relief.

Taking care of ourselves in vulnerable moments helps us not to act out of fear but rather to choose love. Rather than frighten ourselves with runaway thoughts about ourselves and others, we can choose to comfort ourselves with tenderness instead.

With a strong foundation of self-care, we can cultivate the self-respect, honesty and self-awareness we need to grow as people within loving relationships. Forgiving others when we feel we have been wronged, and accepting others' forgiveness when our own hearts require replenishment, is a precious part of giving and receiving in harmony.

Similarly, untreated stress can cause us to speak and act out in regrettable ways towards ourselves and others. Dealing gently but surely with daily stresses involves being attentive to our emotions, needs and itineraries. Living consciously, kindly and carefully allows us to be calmer, happier people. We soon realise that choosing love for ourselves and each other helps us to circumvent stress and conflict both within and around us. Learning profound lessons in relationships over time, we are presented with far fewer challenges in forgiveness and many more moments of joy and peace.

In order to liberate ourselves to live our lives to the fullest, we must free others to do the same. We can forgive ourselves, forgive others, and move forward to embrace the splendour of living lightly. We can release the need to be 'perfect', and loosen our demands upon others to meet our every need and expectation. We are all fallible human beings. When we give ourselves and the ones we love the gift of our forgiveness, we imbue ourselves and others with the motivation and desire to do better in this life. With greater faith and trust in ourselves each day comes the internal fortitude to make more positive decisions.

Learning forgiveness frees us to lead relaxing, powerful and inspiring lives. Practising forgiveness does not mean, however, that we need to settle for behaviour discordant with our own values, directions and dreams. Being discerning in our relationships and decision making involves a loving knowledge of ourselves and our own hearts, made possible by time spent nurturing and caring for our inner world. Our inner world is the world of our emotions, imaginations and instincts. By turning towards ourselves for answers and trusting in ourselves at all times, we need never feel lost or overwhelmed.

Taking the time and care to communicate our thoughts and feelings clearly is emotional intelligence in motion. Nurturing love and forgiveness within ourselves, first and foremost, helps us to know and express ourselves with integrity. Other people sense when we communicate from the heart, as such a language evokes a deeply moving knowingness. At this point and place, spirit to spirit, we meet in humility and honesty. We give ourselves and others the very best chance of understanding and growing through love.

To receive forgiveness is just as powerful as it is to give it. Asking for forgiveness, apologising sincerely, giving and receiving with mutual respect – these are the realities of love. After all, life is long and short. Knowing when to let go and when to hold on is precious intuitive wisdom that comes with consistent practice, faith in ourselves, and the passing of time. In the beautiful words of Sufi mystic Rumi, 'Out beyond ideas of wrongdoing and right-doing there is a field. I'll meet you there. When the soul lies down in that grass the world is too full to talk about.'

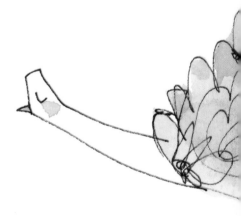

Dear Heart

Thank you for the strength
and the courage
to forgive myself and others
when I am hurt and in pain.

When I feel
that I cannot let go,
help me to open my heart
and surrender to love.

May I forgive myself,
to feel light and free.
May I forgive others,
to end more hurt and pain.

In your infinite wisdom, Heart,
fortify my commitment to love.
Illuminate my way forward
to brighter and higher ground.

As I learn to forgive,
help me to see and feel more joy.

In the peace of forgiveness
show me the bliss
of a lighter, simpler life.

14. LOVE AND INTUITION

As our faith in ourselves blossoms through loving self-care, we come in touch with our own extraordinary intuitive wisdom. Our intuitive voice is the language of our spirit, in perpetual connection with the spirit of love and all things. When we connect with our intuitive wisdom and allow ourselves to be guided by it, we deepen our relationship with ourselves and the power of love that dwells within us. We needn't suspend our conscious thoughts to activate our intuition — rather, we balance and elevate our conscious thoughts with felt 'knowingness' from within. This experience of knowingness is a visceral sense of the flow and rightness of things for us, be they directions, people or decisions that shape our lives. As we listen more carefully and lovingly to ourselves over time, we realise that our intuition is in constant communication with us, supporting us to follow our hearts and travel through life in love.

While some of us may feel less attuned to our intuition than we wish to be, with practice we can develop a swift and dazzling facility in harnessing our natural intuitive faculties. Living instinctually, attuned to our hearts, minds and bodies, is a perfectly organic state of being supportive of our health and happiness. Taking the time to love and care for ourselves each day enables us to develop a wonderfully symbiotic, lifelong relationship with our intuition. We feel ourselves being guided from within to make positive choices that truly delight and nourish us as we live. Indeed, our intuition is inherently loving towards us. It wants to guide us in the direction of peace and joy. All we must do is pay loving attention to our inner wisdom as we move about our daily lives, learning the languages of our own spirits, minds and bodies.

Each time we have a decision to make and feel overwhelmed by choice, even befuddled by a rush of busy thoughts that clouds our clarity, we can quieten down for a moment and place our hands on our hearts. This simple gesture helps to bring us back home within.

At this point we can enjoy a little more peace of mind as we breathe gently and slowly, in and out. Once we feel more settled, breathing steadily and closing our eyes if we please, we can then let the particular question on our mind rest for a moment. We needn't force or expect an answer, rather just let our question settle within us. If we choose, we may even ask ourselves, What would love do?, or What would love say now? … In the quietude of this special moment and the moments following, we may simply allow ourselves to sense what comes to us. We might hear or 'feel' a yes or a no. We might see a picture that helps us to interpret our intuitive wisdom. One thought or vision might nudge forward to highlight itself, illuminating our path.

Coming in touch with the languages of our bodies and feelings also helps us to read important messages from within. Intuitive wisdom is often felt in the form of physical sensations. Sometimes these sensations are subtle, other times overt. As we rest our minds on a particular idea or avenue, we might feel anxious or uneasy. We might notice our breathing begin to feel unsettled, our minds feeling restless or our energy dropping. In contrast, another avenue we consider might soften our bodies into peace. We might notice our hearts being filled with inspiration, our minds and bodies replenished with new energy.

Reading tension and relaxation in our minds and bodies as we connect with ourselves helps us to determine the appropriateness of things for us: to interpret a yes or a no with greater ease and swiftness, and to simply begin to feel what is right for us moving forward. What is right for us might not be right for everyone. Accepting this truth is to live an authentic, intuitive and courageous life in alignment with our own hearts. Importantly, and with due discernment, we can also learn to recognise the difference between the safety of our comfort zone, and all the thoughts and feelings choosing to remain in this space entails, versus the necessary freshness of new adventures we are called to embrace in our lives. This way, we may grow.

Time spent alone helps us to strengthen our intuition, as it is loving attention to ourselves that enables us to cultivate a deeper connection with ourselves and our inner wisdom.

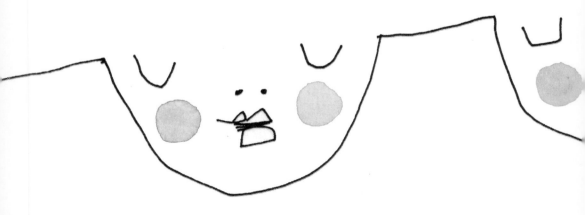

The less noise we have from the outside world, the more we can hear ourselves. As Rumi teaches, in the silence of love, we will find the spark of life. We may find replenishing quietude through meditation of any kind, be that sitting quietly, taking a walk by ourselves, even just closing our eyes for a moment and being peacefully with ourselves.

We may also settle into reflective quiet time doing something that we love: stretching, cooking, reading, perhaps crafting. Switching off from our technologies helps us to exit other stories and realms, and to truly take part in our present moment – our here and now. As such, enjoying time alone without our devices is an important part of self-care. In today's world, we can choose to be surrounded by people, noise and activity at all times. Choosing to spend time alone, and spend time quietly, is a gift to ourselves. It is an elixir for our inner peace, intuitive wisdom and wellness.

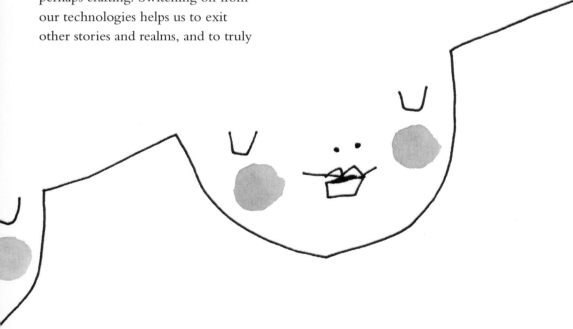

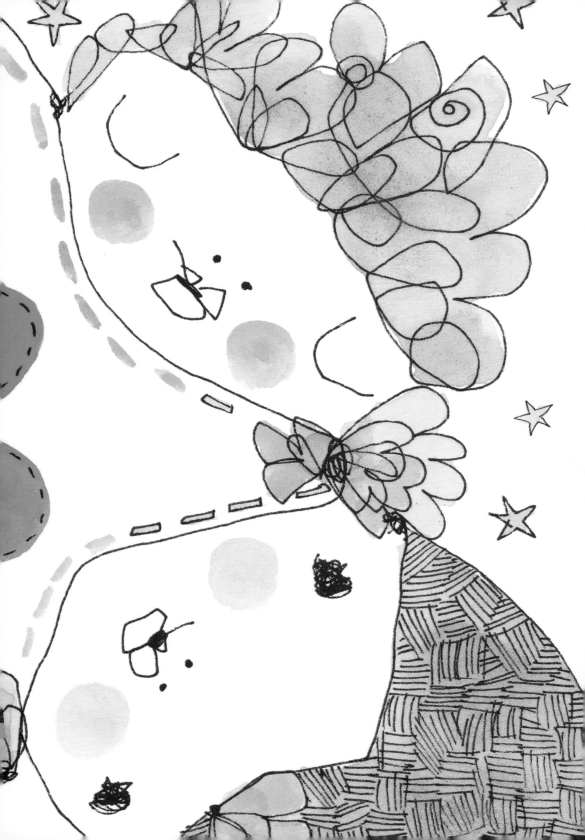

There is a difference between being alone and being lonely. When we are alone in our own loving company, we need never feel lonely. With attention to meeting our own needs, and by granting ourselves permission to express and celebrate our authentic selves, our own company becomes the most joyous and comforting company imaginable. Time spent with ourselves is our own precious time to make and savour. We can sit back in our hearts, make time for conversation with ourselves, and listen in to the gentle, healing wisdom that springs from within us. With the bigger-picture perspective that quietude offers, we see that we always have enough courage and power to choose love – love for ourselves, love for life, and love for one another. When we nourish our hearts in reflective downtime, love embraces us.

Experiencing our intuitive wisdom as a personal wellspring of infinite love grants us tremendous strength and comfort. Upon each path we travel, intuitively guided by love, we are met by an all-encompassing and omniscient energy. There are many words and pictures for this tremendous life force: God, love, nature, universal energy, spirit.

Feeling this loving energy imbues us with all the grace and vitality we need. Indeed, harnessing our intuitive wisdom, we see there is no circumstance or emotion beyond our capacity. Our dedication to daily self-care gifts us the resilience and strength for which we yearn, enabling us to move about our lives with clarity, compassion, self-respect and faith, no matter what may come.

Each time we seek and receive intuitive wisdom, it is important to thank ourselves and life before carrying on with our day. Loving gratitude nourishes our intuition and supports our hearts. We might say or hear the words 'thank you' resound within us as we acknowledge the time we have taken to listen to our own guidance. Indeed, we are nurtured by honouring the wisdom that emerges from within us each moment we choose to access and attend to it. With a very simple practice of quietening down, tuning in to ourselves, allowing what comes and expressing our thanks, we connect with the power of love. This profound and rewarding practice strengthens our intuition, brings us peace, and transforms our experience of life.

Dear Heart

As I spend more time with myself,
help me to hear my inner voice —
a voice brimming with love and wisdom
guiding me on my way.

At every crossroad
remind me to consult my intuition,
trusting in its faithful support
and seeing a clear, loving path ahead.

Thank you for the magic that dwells within me.
I embrace it with all my senses,
sense it in deeply intuitive ways,
and feel it in the love I give and receive.

Help me to be at peace with myself
in gentle moments each day.
Help me to learn the languages
of my body, mind and spirit.

As I experience life in exciting new ways,
let me feel empowered and enriched.
May I honour my intuition
and follow each call to love.

15. LOVE AND BEAUTY

To feel the breath of life on the wind, to capture the fall of a shooting star and to see the spirit of heaven curled into the petals of a flower is to feel the timelessness of beauty — the essence of which invariably stirs our spirits. The beauty of life, so delicate and robust all at once, touches and moves us deeply in each moment we humbly gift our heart's attention to it. In a world of miracles great and small, the moment-to-moment majesty of life positively brims with richness and aliveness to bring us pleasure, intertwine heaven and earth, and satiate our lifelong appetite for enchantment. By choosing love, we choose to see the beauty in all things. Life, in its omniscience, wisdom and flow, offers us enduring nourishment and boundless inspiration; we need only choose to see it. Beauty draws us in and uplifts us. Beauty speaks to our hearts. When we yearn to make things beautiful, to see the beauty in ourselves and one another, and to be appreciative of the sublime earth that surrounds us, we may lead deeply loving lives that truly illuminate and expand our hearts.

Through infinite creative expressions of romance, euphoria, grief, loss and hope, love stories continue to be told, from artistic, architectural and botanical masterpieces to literary, musical, even culinary offerings inspired by all kinds of love. Palatial structures of religious devotion pepper our planet, reaching for the clouds and inspiring our awe. Portraits painted with a brush moved by hands of desire, yearning and love reveal themselves in cheeky gazes spanning the history of art. Breathtaking, romantic poetry can leave sublime stanzas floating through our hearts; moving love songs echo our pain and joy. Frances Hodgson Burnett's bittersweet tale *The Secret Garden* tells of a beautiful, natural sanctuary touched by unthinkable grief and loss. This locked-away, secret garden is ultimately overgrown beyond recognition, only to be rediscovered with new life and new joy — a metaphor of love itself.

In devotional expressions of creativity, we see ourselves and each other. Appreciating stories, our own and others', we deepen our respect for the feelings that inspire and motivate us all to express what is felt and known within, oftentimes even creating great beauty from the depths of our loss and pain. Indeed, in weary-hearted moments, choosing love means choosing to see the beauty of life. The beauty we see around us is the beauty that dwells within us, reflected and returned to us in boundless ways. In this sense, our experiences of beauty, like a balm for our spirits, fortify us.

When we see the beauty in life and love life, we naturally bring love to all we do and, living so, create beauty on earth in our own unique ways. In his powerful teaching on the subject of work, Kahlil Gibran's prophet speaks of doing our life's work, whatever that work may be, with love, describing work as 'love made visible'. Indeed, speaks the prophet, if we cannot do our work with love, we are best to wait at the doors of the temple and take alms from those who work with love, lest we muddy the waters of life with our diminished perspective and begrudging effort.

Beauty is celebrated and regenerated by the time and care we take to embrace life and translate the inspiration we receive into thoughts, words and acts of love. These acts may be simple: a cup of tea prepared with intention, a cake decorated with love, a bed made with care or a thoughtful visit to a friend. They may also be grand: the passionate conducting of an orchestra or a gallant declaration of romance. All things can be done, and made beautiful, with love.

The beauty of life blossoms and grows as our vision grows and blossoms. This bodes delightfully well for us as we move through our lives, learning, growing and cultivating our gratitude over time so that all things are felt by us as miracles. So that each day is enjoyed to the fullest. So that the splendour of life simply cannot pass us by. Our hearts, surrendered and softened to the beauty of love, become porous to the joys of life.

So touched we can become by the beauty of life that the flight of a butterfly, the lightness of a snowflake in hand, the embrace of a loved one or the warmth of an honest smile can bring us to tears. In our tears of joy, our love flows.

Nurturing an inner world in which all feelings are welcomed – in which lightness, spontaneity, compassion and tenderness find their rightful home – we are able to see with unbridled loving vision. We even grow our heart's capacity to hold, feel, absorb and reflect all the more beauty through love. To love life is to raise our hands to the sky in equal measures of gratitude and humility, appreciating all that we feel, have and know, while acknowledging life's inherent grace, mystery and inexplicable beauty.

The divine spirit of life that moves through each of us is the spirit of all things: a potent, creative and beautiful life force.

To be beautiful is to be ourselves, stripped of all pretence, released of old density and pain, with hearts upon our sleeves and spirits set free at last. To be ourselves is to gift ourselves, others and life the natural love and beauty we by birthright possess. Circling with the flow of life as we meet each moment and season with love, we may feel awakened again and again by the warmth of sun kissing our skin, the changing leaves of autumn, the blush of a cheek, the taste of fruit from a vine, a tender look from loving eyes, and the sheer, limitless beauty of life.

Dear Heart

In life's beauty I come alive.

May I feel my spirit touched and swayed
by boundless love within and around me.
May life become all the more heavenly with my loving effort,
and may my appreciation for living allow my joy to blossom.

In moments in which I feel weary, dear Heart,
may endless beauty fill you with inspiration,
breathing into you
the promise of new hope and life.

May the touch of loved ones,
the essence of nature
and the beauty of little things
always find pathways to your ever open door.

As I open my eyes wide to love,
may I see natural beauty in myself and others.
May I avail all my senses to the beauty of life
and feel enriched by love forever more.

16. LOVE AND ROMANCE

Romance in love is expressive of tenderness and care, sensuality and passion. True romance takes thoughtfulness and is inspired by a desire for deep connection — a yearning to delight, know and nurture one another deeply. Romantic love can be as soothing and cosy as it is thrilling, hypnotic, wild and free. Indeed, and at its best, romantic love is all these wonderful things and more: a delicious, enriching melange of feelings, experiences, words, acts and sublime moments of togetherness. Living romantically is an art and a way of life. Nurtured upon a grounding foundation of mutual respect and adoration, spontaneity and desire can play and blossom. Romantic love inspires happiness and gifts us with strength, comfort and pleasure. As the heavenly treats of romance nourish our hearts, we feel our senses awaken.

The way lovers come together on earth is both beautiful and mysterious. Divine timing seems to have a great deal to do with our fortuitous meetings – meetings that can bedazzle and enchant us for a lifetime. The lessons we are meant to learn in this life, the people to whom we are drawn, what we see in each other and what we can give and receive in romantic love are all part of our unique journeys into self-discovery, learning and growth. Romantic love can transport us, taking us to new heights at which our disbelief and resistance are necessarily suspended. At such heights, we embrace love as a celebration of our lives. Not all romances are meant to last – a painful truth in the way of love, and a reality with which most of us are deeply familiar. Yet, with good faith, presence and awareness, we can come together lovingly and leave each other richer than when we first united, if not stay together for a lifetime.

Some say that our romances are written into the design of our lives before we are even born – that there are no coincidences or chance meetings, only divine plans. These divine plans include the people we meet, when and where they will be met, and how the love we share will manifest over time. They detail the many adventures that will bring colour and meaning to our rich, earthly lives. Philosophising upon a predetermined path of life is not to disempower us, nor to detract from our individual liberty and will. We are and always will be at the helms of our stories, thinking thoughts and taking actions that shape our worlds moment to moment. Yet a divine plan for our lives has its own kind of intelligence. An intelligence that, when met with our respect, constantly inspires new depths of humility, gratitude and wonder. Trusting in the beauty, serendipity and perfection of life's plan when it comes to finding and relishing our rightful path in love gifts us with immense peace and joy.

Sometimes love can take time. We can acquaint ourselves in a courtship, familiarising ourselves with one another, and, little by little, falling in love. 'Love at first sight' speaks to a knowingness that we can possess about somebody – a beloved companion who, just moments before, may have appeared to us as a stranger. In the words of Sufi mystic Rumi, 'Lovers don't finally meet

somewhere, they are in each other all along.' This sentiment shines light upon the euphoric familiarity we can sense in the presence of another human being who, without even saying a word, seems to arrest us with love and see us completely. As if looking through and beyond our eyes, our beloved instantaneously forgoes any minutia, instead clearing a path directly to our heart by way of our spirit. The gravitas of a single moment in love can change an entire life. The pure energy of two spirits in direct conversation seals a union, transcending the conscious mind and physical body. In such an instance and by such a miracle, we are changed. We find ourselves with one foot in heaven, the other on earth.

The idea of 'falling' in love suggests a kind of surrender – an experience in which we let go, let life happen, and let our feelings be felt. The all-encompassing, compelling nature of falling into romantic love draws us into the immediacy and intensity of the present moment – the only moment we truly have, and the only moment in which all possibilities become available to us. In this way, romantic love makes us feel truly and completely alive.

In its various iterations, all of which are deeply meaningful, romantic love changes and evolves over time. With due care, changing and evolving love needn't be confused with lost love. At the beginning of a romance, the fire of love can burn particularly brightly, vivid with sparks of freshness and intensity. Contrary to popular belief, early passion in our love stories needn't necessarily dwindle over time. With mutual attention and care, tenderness and desire in romantic love can be limitless. For many lovers, however, the bedazzlement of early desire can settle over time, with comfiness and steadiness becoming more important and valuable qualities in love. Even still, romance needn't become less significant, enriching or compelling over time. Rather, ever-blossoming romances may be experienced among, even shaped by, the ebbs, flows, surprises and delights of togetherness in enduring companionship. As we awaken to the beauty of living and gift our full presence to daily life, the endless possibilities for joy and romance awaiting us become available, tantalising and utterly impossible to miss.

In today's world, a fast-moving world in which most things are replaceable and gratification can be instant, we are wise to keep romantic love precious, if not (and possibly at best) a little old fashioned. We are wise not to underestimate the value of chivalry, the power of genuine effort, and the gifts of compassion and patience. We must see our beloveds as individuals growing and changing over time, just as fallible, splendid, vulnerable and alive as we are. We cannot enter into a romance wishing to change somebody in order to find happiness. Rather, we must enter into a romance choosing to love and respect our beloved, and choose them with love each day. Romance requires generosity of spirit in loving relationships. It involves the expression of gratitude, never taking one another for granted, and co-creating supportive, peaceful and sustainable unions that are brave and agile in the face of inevitable change.

Lasting romance is a co-creative pleasure that celebrates the learning of love's languages. Cultivating romantic love in our daily lives requires attention to detail, gratitude and understanding.

In his popular work *The Five Love Languages*, Gary Chapman outlines our unique ways of expressing and experiencing love, helping us to better nourish ourselves and the ones we love. For some, physical gifts are signs of romantic love and care. A bunch of roses, a box of chocolates or perhaps some beautiful lingerie signify that we are adored. For others, quality time is of greatest value in love: doing things together and spending time side by side. For some, affirmative, loving speech is particularly powerful. For such people, hearing the words I love you and receiving genuine, thoughtful words of loving encouragement matter most. For some lovers, thoughtful acts of service make all the difference. The offer of a helping hand, working together and sharing responsibilities: the initiative and teamwork affectionate companionship entails may be experienced by such lovers as true romance. For others, touch is the most expressive, romantic, intimate and meaningful language in love.

While some love languages may seem less racy and more practical than others, all feed into romantic love. We must remember that lasting love is not stoked in a single moment, but nurtured across the course of a whole day or, indeed, an entire lifetime. The art of making love does not speak solely to the act of making physical love. Rather, love is a way of being – romance, a way of life. We can bring a sense of romance to all we are and do, beginning with the way we see things. Seeing the beauty around us, harnessing that beauty, allowing it to infuse our spirits and tint our vision with romance, makes us greater lovers – more in touch with our own sensuality and the sensuality of life. Our sensuality may be experienced in the way we communicate and take care of ourselves, the way we dress, even the way we bring a feeling of intimacy and romance to our homes and environments. Choosing to live romantically helps to imbue our relationships with the passion, energy and freshness they require to flourish.

Each and every one of us deserves to have our senses awakened by romance – to feel adored, and sense our minds, bodies and spirits tickled and ignited by love. We also deserve to know that it is possible to feel and savour romance as long as we live. A thoughtful touch, a beautifully placed compliment, a carefully planned adventure, a gorgeous room, a certain look – in all these delicious, tactile, tender and unforgettable moments, we come to know and relish romance in love.

The more romantic we are, the richer, more intimate and beautiful our lives become. Choosing to lead romantic lives, we may truly delight and nourish our hearts.

Dear Heart

Thank you for the joy of romance in my life.
Help me to nourish my romantic self
and nurture my relationships with tenderness
so that I may feel inspired, adored and alive.

May I take the time and care
to explore creative expressions of love.
May learning about love's ways nourish me
and help me to give more deeply and fully.

At any time love finds me overwhelmed
or when I feel lonely or unloved,
restore my faith in life's divine plan for me.
Nurture me with comfort, and help me on my way.

In your gentle wisdom, Heart,
please remind me just how loveable I am.
I am worthy and complete,
and I am ready for love.

The love I am seeking is seeking me.
May it come to light up my world
and reveal to me all the delights
of a truly romantic life.

17. LOVE AND LETTING GO

Knowing when to hold on to or let go of love, especially in romantic relationships, is a delicate art involving self-awareness, sensitivity, courage and faith. By drawing on our intuitive wisdom, making a concerted effort to nurture our relationships in daily life, and taking heed of lessons learnt in love, we may naturally come to sense when to hold on to, and when to let go of, love.

Falling in love, and being in love with our beloved, it is often inconceivable to consider that one day, such a love should end. And rightly so; it is by entering into our chosen romances confidently and passionately, with full faith in love, that we live fully. Letting go of a love that has touched us deeply can feel devastating – be we the ones to actively let go of such love, or the ones to be let go. We may feel overwhelmed by the decision-making processes in separation, burdened by confusion, doubt or guilt; we may even feel fearful of an uncertain future. In love, we build our lives around one another. The loss of routine, common ground, shared environments and shared relationships can leave us feeling terrible sadness. We may not know how to move forward, nor how to relearn ways of being and identifying ourselves outside partnership. However, if and when the time comes to let go of a relationship, realising that our love stories continue – that our lives can and do go on – is profoundly empowering.

In our romantic relationships we may reach a point at which the proverbial 'thrill' is gone; in which we no longer feel delight, interest, tenderness or affection. We simply cannot make our hearts feel things they do not. Nothing of great noteworthiness may have occurred, yet we are struck by a feeling of separateness or loss: a sense of disconnection beyond repair. This difficult feeling may be mutual or unrequited. Countless romances meet an end in a natural way, even if effort has been made to mend, grow, and make things work together. In such instances, true grace, courage and sensitivity are required in the letting go of love. A mutually respectful parting honours a shared love story, acknowledges the depth of feelings, and pays tribute to the end of one era and the beginning of another. Such a parting is made possible by clear, honest communication, compassion, and thoughtfulness. Even if our dignified approach to parting ways is not met by our beloved, it is always our choice to stay aligned with our own hearts and values. Letting go of a precious romance with respect, in the spirit with which it began, we may, at the very least, nourish our own hearts as we move forward in peace.

All romantic love can be challenged by tension, disagreement and difference. Even the most amorous and harmonious of partners can find themselves sparring, especially when stressed and weary, and often about the littlest of things. Friction and conflict can work in functional ways, clearing the air between lovers and making way for deeper understanding. We are cautioned, however, to understand that there is no place for nastiness, aggression, dishonesty and disrespect in true love. True love is not a game. No scores are to be kept, nor are we to be played, abused, manipulated or taken for granted in loving partnership. If we are to experience any such harmful or hurtful behaviour, we are prudent to let go of our beloveds with self-compassion, and our self-preservation, at heart.

We are wiser to be alone, in powerful, nurturing relationships with ourselves and life, than to be in any relationship, romantic or otherwise, that takes from our peace and joy. In good faith, we must trust that our partner will learn and grow too, through their conscious process of separation and renewal.

Sometimes letting go of love can come as a great relief, especially at the end of a difficult relationship, and particularly in instances in which both lovers can see the value in parting ways. In such circumstances, we may find ourselves being able to let go and move on more easily. Sometimes letting go of love makes way for unexpected relief.

We might not have realised how hard it was to be holding on to something that wasn't right for us, and, in the letting go of it, we feel infinitely better. We feel stronger, calmer and more comfortable within ourselves and our lives than before. In other situations, the reality of a separation may come to us as a debilitating shock. We may feel as if a carpet has been pulled from beneath us. We may endeavour with all our strength to rebuild and recover our confidence and desire for life, though we lack energy, and feel overwhelmed by our emotions.

We might be met with a dizzying mix of joyous and difficult memories as we relive moments shared. Everything we see, hear, read, eat or think reminds us of our beloveds, and we feel utterly demoralised.

After a painful letting go of love, we are called to find our peace, confidence and zest for life again. The greatest healer – aside from love itself, which is always within, around and ahead of us – is time.

We can begin by making the time to be with and nurture ourselves. We can be generous with this time, not hurrying ourselves to move on before we have had a chance to rest, grieve, feel our feelings and pledge to replenish our hearts. Surrounding ourselves with wonderful people whose company we love brings us comfort and joy when we need a lift. Committing to exiting our hermitage and experiencing the outside world gifts us with fresh stimulation and perspective. Bolstering our moods, hearts and immune systems with exercise, funny movies, nourishing foods, time in nature, good hydration, uplifting music and gentle self-care rituals contributes to our healing, as does seeking help when needed. Little by little we begin to emerge from our sadness, and our hearts start to feel a little stronger.

To be courageous in any stage of love, we must trust that life will carry us into new chapters with perfect timing. Indeed, there is not a single moment of our lives in which we are not being held by great love. In our darkest, most challenging moments, keeping faith in love to look after us can take immense strength. Yet, the rewards of choosing to believe in love outweigh the pain of losing our faith in its power. Every one of us can learn to love again with integrity and willingness, no matter what we may have endured. We can begin new chapters and create bountiful futures drawing on our dreams. We can never quite know what delightful surprises life has in store for us, nor underestimate the beauty of a rainbow after a storm.

Our experiences in love teach us so much. Even when our lessons in love are painful, they are still gifts that contribute to growing our unique wisdom. Consciously experiencing the challenges, highs and lows of love while nourishing our hearts in daily life, we may learn to cultivate greater trust in ourselves, life, and love. Our ability to be courageous, and to be accepting of things as they are, is strengthened by deeper insight. We see that love meant forever will endure, while other loves not meant for us over time will organically dissolve or pass us by. Learning to listen to our hearts empowers us to know what to do at all times, and supports us to move with confidence and grace through all stages and seasons of love.

Dear Heart

You and I know the pain of love;
we also know the joy.
While joy may come and go in love,
the richness of love is forever.

Bolster me with courage
when I need to let go
of a love that no longer feels right.

Imbue me with bravery
when a love I wish not to end
demands I let go.

Help me to trust in love again
and in your own strength, Heart.
Indeed, while I can underestimate you,
you are potent and powerful beyond words.

May I feel the peace of freedom
and wish the same peace for those I love.
May I express myself honestly
and encourage those I love to do the same.

When it comes to moving forward
fortify me with each step.
Help me to nourish you deeply
as I welcome a bright new beginning.

18. LOVE, RESISTANCE AND HEALING

Love knows no bounds and possesses miraculous healing powers. Giving and receiving love can imbue us with new life, make us glow, soothe our hurries and worries, and bring vitality to our bodies, comfort to our minds, and softness and beauty to our faces. Yet it is curious that love, all inspiring as it is, can be something that we resist, be that wittingly or unwittingly. Indeed, when it comes to love, we are usually the ones to stand in our very own way of happiness. Let us explore how this could be so, and discover more conscious ways of living in which we open our hearts fully to healing love.

Too often we find ourselves completely unaware of our unique splendour. Pride and vanity are quite different to healthy self-esteem and self-respect — virtues well worth cultivating for life. And given that our subconscious minds have no sense of humour, self-deprecating self-talk can have catastrophic effects on our quality of living — our inner peace and joie de vivre. With a personal foundation of loving self-care, we grow our sense of worthiness, realising that we are indeed enough. We always were, we presently are, and, moving forward, we always will be enough. It is very important that we interrupt sabotaging thoughts of inadequacy and replace them with better-quality thoughts. It is a tragic loss for ourselves and others when we stifle our creativity and live half-lives built on a lack of faith in ourselves. Courage to see our strength and boldly embody the fullness of our potential — our aliveness — is to live passionately and powerfully in a state of love.

We may have once been told by another person that we lack in some way and, as a result, feel unworthy of being loved just as we are. We might then find it hard to accept when other people love us just as

we are, including all the bits we ourselves might find a little odd or unusual. We might accidentally get ruffled by such unconditional love and inadvertently turn it away with insecure and confusing behaviour. In effect, we stand in love's way, after which we often feel more unlovable. This strange yet remarkably common behavioural pattern is worthy of our attention. By nourishing our own hearts, we begin to remedy and positively reimagine our ways of being. The more we love, accept and treasure ourselves, the more others will be able to love and treasure us.

As well as unhelpful commentary from those with whom we share our lives, the media with which we engage might be unsuitable for us, draining us with messages of lack and causing us to question ourselves, body, mind and spirit. Intelligent enjoyment of media is crucial for our happiness, as is general discernment in our interpersonal relationships. While constructive criticism can be very powerful if delivered tactfully and received with grace, and self-improvement is very exciting territory, we are wise to realise that our own self-opinion is of the greatest consequence.

Our self-opinion is the basis of our wellbeing, and shapes all the relationships we will ever nurture in this life. We simply must not allow the opinions, tastes or influences of others to uproot or diminish us. We are all worthy of happiness, inner peace and love. Knowing ourselves and building loving, trusting bonds with ourselves for life, we find ourselves all the wiser, happier and more resilient. We stop standing in our own way and in the way of love, letting life flow freely in serendipity.

Other fascinating untruths in which we can find ourselves utterly entangled include believing that love is for others but not for us; that love cannot last; that there isn't enough love for us; that we simply cannot be happy, loved and loveable; or that a real love story blossoming on our path of life is quite simply just too good to be true. We might have had one painful or unsuccessful relationship and declare that all our future amorous adventures will follow suit. We may have heard stories of love and pain that influence our own myths and cause us to feel suspicious or disbelieving in the goodness of love and life. Yet life is a magical journey at the heart of which is love. Limiting our belief in love by choosing to think in cynical, restrictive ways devoid of romanticism, faith and self-belief assures us lives of discontent. We will always feel as if we are missing out on something and that happiness is eluding us. Choosing love means choosing to believe in its sublime magic, surrendering to it, and letting it heal and nourish our hearts. Letting more love in allows us to feel, see and know more love, as love is kinetic and ever evolving. We needn't change overnight. Taking little steps in love's direction, we may begin. As we start to flourish in love's miraculous light, it behoves us to meet our bliss with heartfelt joy and gratitude.

In the power of loving prayer and delightfully documented stories of spontaneous healings, saints and angels, love finds its home among a smorgasbord of mesmerising miracles. Love has been known to turn lives around, even to save them: its holiness and sacred power a force beyond compare. When we send loving thoughts to ourselves, one another and nature, we become part of a healing energy on earth. The more attuned we become to love, the more a part of this tremendous energy we feel and the more energised we naturally become. By living conscious, creative, passionate stories aligned with our hearts, and completely in love with life, we satiate our curiosity for the power of love and our desire to contribute lovingly.

In a spirit of openness to love, loving relationships meant for us will be seeking us as we seek them. The less resistant and more acquainted we become with love, the more easily we will be able to read what is truly right, healing and nourishing for us. The loving respect we show ourselves will set the tone for others to treat us in loving ways that enliven, enrich and honour us.

We must permit ourselves to love, and feel loved and loveable. We must know that there is plenty of love on earth, more than enough to make us happy, and that the energy of love is perpetually growing and flourishing within and around us. We must believe that we are inherently more than enough, just as we are, and learn to praise, comfort and delight ourselves with loving thoughts that replenish our hearts. We must celebrate room for improvement in our lives, as such room only makes space for us to experience more peace and joy. We must know that our thoughts and self-talk create our worlds, and that by positively transforming them, we transform our lives. We must trust that we have the means and the freedom to love, and cultivate the courage not only to overcome our resistance to love, but to believe in it as long as we live.

Dear Heart

May all my resistance to love
melt into this moment.
May I breathe deeply
and open my eyes.

May the miracle of love
within and around me
imbue me with an endless
awareness of magic.

May love's healing power
touch my thoughts,
my speech and my actions.
May I feel at home in love's way.

Each time I question myself, Heart,
please return me swiftly back to love.
May I embrace myself in this moment
as I watch all my dreams come true.

19. LOVE, RESILIENCE AND CHANGE

Cultivating resilience in the face of change — the only constant in our lives — and learning the art of non-attachment to things, outcomes and ideas is a gift to ourselves. Choosing love and living lovingly anchors us so that we may possess the courage, optimism, and compassion towards ourselves and others required to transcend preconceived ideas or judgements about how life 'should' be. As we open our hearts, we open our minds to infinite possibilities, and to seeing beyond what we already know. Living in inclusive, non-judgemental ways frees us to live creative, intuitive lives supportive of our personal and collective wellbeing. We create our realities and the stories we tell ourselves and others about who we are and how we live. By choosing love as our lives change daily, we connect with the full potential, magic and depth of our human experience in which nothing is permanent, and in which it is always the right time to be open and blossom.

In his wonderful and profound little book *The Book of Tea*, Japanese author Kakuzo Okakura writes that the art of life lies in a constant readjustment to our surroundings. Indeed, it is a tremendous paradox that change is our only constant in life. We are ever-changing beings in a constantly shifting world. We change age, opinion, geography, ideas, style, jobs, relationships and more. It is no wonder that amid endless change and flux we try to control what we can, or think we can, in order to feel some comfort and stability. We can resist change, close our hearts and feel confronted or even daunted by it. Perceiving change and the unknown as insecure and risky territory in life inevitably depletes and stresses us. While change can evoke fear and uncertainty, choosing to open our hearts to newness allows us to discover the many wonderful surprises and adventures that await us. In the comfort and security of our own unconditional love, we have all the bravery and strength we need to feel safe as we move forward in life.

Self-care practices support our hearts to feel secure in a changing world, assisting us to stop scaring ourselves with troublesome, worrying thoughts, and flourish beyond our comfort zones. We can replace questions of 'What could go wrong?' with 'What could go right … ?' In doing so, we welcome new conversations about serendipity, smooth transitions, and dreams coming true. Alan Watts wrote that the only way to make sense of change is to plunge into it, move with it, and join the dance. When we realise that the dance of life will and does go on, irrespective of our procrastination or reluctance to join it, we begin to see that our willingness to embrace change delivers the love, peace and joy we seek. Life is in perpetual motion, with its own magical rhythm designed to carry us. All we need to do is join the dance.

We all need and yearn for love and connection, yet profound philosophy, including that of Zen Buddhism, suggests that happiness has a lot to do with non-attachment. How can we make sense of this idea, when love seems to inevitably involve our desire to know, possess, have and hold somebody, some place or some thing? People, places and things are never guaranteed; they spontaneously change, come and go. Taoist philosopher Lao Tzu cited resistance to change as a major cause of our daily human suffering and sorrow, suggesting that, in contrast, by allowing things to flow naturally forward as they do, we may tap into a wellspring of calm and contentment. Living this idea consciously, we may transform our lives and grow stronger as we navigate the various challenges with which change can present us.

Exploring the notion of love and non-attachment more deeply, we may notice that while love is the greatest energetic force on earth, there is also so much lovelessness in circulation. As we clutch onto

desires and expectations – often out of greed and fear – lovelessness manifests, severing our connections with one another and, at worst, dulling our faith in life. We become very poor when we lose our faith in love and life, and when we focus on our own gains and happiness at the expense of others. We become very rich when we choose to live fully and believe in love, and when the joy, success and peace of others feels just as important as our own.

Stability in our hearts derives from a bigger-picture awareness of love – love that goes beyond the physical, material world and that is a matter of profound, all-encompassing energy.

Love is unto itself perfectly complete. The experience of love in our changing lives and changing world is about a certain state or quality of being – thought, feeling and connection – a state or quality that is timeless, infinitely flexible and ever evolving. Focusing on the essence of our lived experience of love beyond any fixed agenda or any object of our affection, we are more gracefully able to embrace change and navigate the natural coming and going of things.

Writer Anais Nin wrote that there comes a time when the risk it takes to stay tightly held like a bud eclipses the risk it takes to blossom. In the constant flux of life, we can be swept up and hold tightly to our many reasons for not joining the dance and flourishing. We might think tomorrow will be our day, next week, next month, or next year – perhaps, even, never. But, the time to embrace change and blossom is now, just as a tiny bud changes over time and naturally turns into a beautiful flower.

And it does so without self-consciousness: not comparing itself to any other flower, but blossoming because it is its natural design to do so, just as it is ours. By practising non-attachment to material outcomes, not holding on to stifling expectations, not living as a means to an end, but rather living to live and to nourish our hearts, we discover a whole new way of being.

As we learn to celebrate, support and connect with ourselves, each other and nature through our open-heartedness, we flourish together. And flourishing together through love is what our world needs now, more than ever.

Dear Heart

In the midst of constant change
you are my trusted anchor.
Sunshine, rain or stormy skies,
let us navigate life in a sea of love.

In this sea where waves come and go,
may I find peaceful ways
to let go of all things
as they naturally change and grow.

Help me to love without expectations.
Help me to receive love in peace and joy.
Show me the courage to join the dance of life,
and learn new steps with a smile as I go.

In the knowingness that love
is all and everything,
may I savour inspiration and solace
each day of my life.

20. LOVE AND ONENESS

There is something fascinating about the way we experience our humanity in connection with one another and in connection with ourselves and life. The fascinating bond that we share with all creation is at certain moments very deeply felt in our hearts. An arrestingly beautiful encounter in nature. The warmth of a loved one's embrace in which we feel at one. Looking into the eyes of a beloved pet with a profound sense of understanding beyond words. Such experiences of connection and unity seem to bring us a very particular sense of peace and joy — a sense we recognise and for which we deeply yearn: a feeling of being at home at last. These precious moments can feel fleeting, yet, with attunement, self-awareness and gratitude, we can learn to cultivate and enjoy a blissful state of oneness over the entire course of our lifetimes. To live in this way is essentially to live in a state of love in which there is no disconnection or separateness; there is quite simply oneness and wholeness of which we are an intrinsic and organic part.

Love touches us all, surrounding and enlivening us. Invisible love is constantly teaching and tickling us, imbuing us with strength, wisdom, comfort and joy. The all-encompassing nature of love speaks to its divine, endless and omniscient quality. Indeed, love is a sea of energy in which we all flow – a way of life in which we all belong, and into which we are all welcomed.

In a spirit of love, we can do so many things. Love is grand, healing, playful and rejuvenating. Love replenishes our hearts and strengthens us, body, mind and spirit. With a little time and care, we naturally begin to see that we are fragments of one great love in motion, moving about individually each day yet woven by the very same cloth. We are all – and always – interconnected, and by choosing love we choose the joy of life. We cultivate happiness, inclusivity and respect for ourselves, each other and our earth and, in doing so, we all blossom.

We spend much of our lives feeling terribly separate from each other, nature and the miracle of life due to the way we are taught to see and experience things as separate, or 'other'. We compete and compare, measuring ourselves against others in all too often unhelpful and unproductive ways. We also busy ourselves with labels and the accumulation of things to define and differentiate us. In our various attempts to feel loveable, happy and worthy, we often find ourselves losing touch with ourselves, each other and the inherent abundance of life. The more united and connected we allow ourselves to feel in love, the happier, healthier and richer we become. The more we seek to care for, understand and harmonise with one another and life, the more connected, inspired and alive we feel. By opening our minds to the oneness of love, we live our lives to nourish our hearts.

Living with a sense of the oneness of love helps us to practise compassion with ourselves and others. What we do unto others, we do unto ourselves. Appreciating this truth helps us to navigate our lives and relationships with more kindness and care. With an awareness of constant love within and around us, we also awaken to the magic of life and the infinite creative possibilities that surround us at all times. We feel love encouraging us at every turn, wanting us to feel peace and joy. As we journey on, we begin to see that choosing love gifts us with the richness and beauty of life. Awakening to this reality, we are compelled to choose love as a way of being.

Embracing love's oneness, we also begin to see ourselves as part of a collective on a shared journey of life, rather than as isolated individuals charting our own territory for our own means and ends. With this awareness, we are inspired to explore more possibilities for collaboration and contribution, working together to make a difference: celebrating and elevating each other rather than comparing and competing with one another. As we change the way we see things, things change.

Our growing faith in connection and the goodness of love will naturally gift us with more nourishing, supportive connections of all kinds, transforming our lives in radical ways. Coming to daily life with a knowingness that there is enough for everyone, and with a spirit of community and cooperation, we find ourselves to be happier people leading brighter, more meaningful lives.

Living with an awareness of the oneness of love also supports us to feel at home within ourselves, and in the worlds in which we live. We are constantly reminded that we are never alone. Indeed, one conversation, one touch or one perfect moment can restore our hearts completely, reminding us of our timeless connection to all life through the power, portal and peace that is love.

Let us take a moment to reflect on the linear time–space continuum upon which we interpret and organise our daily lives into increments, hour to hour, day by day, month by month in our calendar years. The way we measure in millimetres and metres, acres, miles and yards. These systems and structures by which we live in modern life are for the most part accepted as natural and normal, yet they are human designs. We created such constructs and continue to live by them.

Curiously, various traditions and cultures around the world have a different sense of the way time and space can be measured and experienced. The ancient Vedic worldview is circular, and is understood in cycles of birth, death, and rebirth. We experience lifetime after lifetime, returning to learn the lessons we didn't learn in previous lifetimes, and experience the wondrous journeys still awaiting us. In Indigenous Australian culture, the term 'Dreamtime' refers to the past, present and future. By this wonderful worldview, moments and places old, new and yet to come can occupy a shared space and time. People, events and stories of the past intermingle with the present moment, and with hopes, dreams and visions for the future, to create a fulsome experience of life.

We can all learn from other ways of seeing and experiencing time and space, informing and enhancing our own reality, and deepening our understanding of life and love. We can embrace a mix of memories from the past, physical and visceral experiences, thoughts and feelings in the present moment, and merge awareness of these elements with an activation of our intuitive faculties about what is yet to come: the beauty, love and joy of life that still await us.

Living with a more expansive, co-creative and curious sense of life, old, new and emerging, love becomes part of a greater and grander story in which the energy of love is what is most important, and something that we can never lose. We can never lose a love we have had in the past, because the energy of love is something that is continually re-creating, re-birthing, re-constituting, re-making itself in our present moment and future lives, beyond measurement by any structure of time and space. So just like time, which is in itself paradoxically and essentially timeless, love can be seen as an energy or a force that exists beyond time, and that is boundless in nature.

As we deepen our curiosity here, we are compelled to consider the life of our own unique spirits and the life of the spirit world: those in spirit with whom we walk. The people or creatures we think of might have passed into spirit, or exited our day-to-day lives. There is a tremendously awe-inspiring pool of thought worthy of our consideration: that there isn't another dimension, so to speak, in which those in spirit exist, nor do they depart forever. Rather, the spirit world shares the same dimension as ours. We are coexisting in one time and space, and the access point for us to reach all love and life is any moment in which the veil between us and all else thins: in which we don't see ourselves as separate to nature, creatures, each other or loved ones past, present and future. Rather, we feel ourselves at one with the spirit of life on a shared plane – as part of a shared story and energy of love.

When we allow our hearts to soften and open, we connect with this shared knowingness: one love. We sense our belonging to the spirit of life, and we feel bliss. We needn't access another dimension to feel the oneness of love; the dimension is here and now: a shared dimension open and accessible to each and every one of us.

228

These ideas may seem esoteric and philosophical, maybe even grandiose. And yet they are possibly, at their very roots, the simplest, most profound philosophies of life: that we are one, that we share a spirit of life, and that we are all energy – moving, shaking, vibrating, expanding, contracting, dancing energy.

Our separateness is an illusion, just as life is but a dream. In this awareness, we come home. And as we come home, we realise that our home is love.

Dear Heart

Thank you for gifting me
with a curiosity to explore love.
I am nourished by all that I know
and humbled by that which I have yet to learn.

In my daily life let me feel
precious moments of deep connection.
Remind me of my belonging to love:
to one spirit of life.

As I see myself in others and others in me,
may my heart soften and open.
May the love within and around me
shape each moment of my life.

May those I love in spirit
walk close beside me,
letting me feel their presence
and sharing in my joy.

Fill me with fresh inspiration
as I explore new ideas and feelings.
Let my spirit float freely in love
and let me dance my way through life.

CLOSING NOTES

Embarking upon a moment-to-moment, day-to-day journey into love as a lifelong commitment is quite possibly the point and purpose of our being. Connecting with our hearts in daily life, listening to and following their lead, takes and grows our courage. As we create our own stories about ourselves and our lives, we engage our creativity, sensitivity and intuition. Actively choosing to see ourselves, others and life with love, we imbue ourselves with the power of peace and the gentle confidence of true strength from within.

Choosing love through all the seasons of our lives, we connect with the full potential, magic and depth of our human experience. In her beautiful poem 'Mindful', Mary Oliver describes a rich and endless process of learning made possible for us as we choose to look within, listen carefully, and lose ourselves within a soft world. Indeed, love shows us a soft world in which infinite lessons may nurture and enrich our spirits for life. In choosing love, we come to see far beyond what we could ever know, traversing brave, bright and sublime new territory.

In an ever-changing world, our loving self-care practices can support our hearts to feel safe. While everything around us is in endless flux, through love we can become more ourselves with each new day. Non-attachment has much to do with our health and happiness. Learning to nurture our hearts so that we may detach, yet love fully, is true wisdom and freedom. As the mystic Osho teaches, love begins where fear ends. Learning to love and be loved, to love and let go, to love and trust in life, we may be both discerning and open-hearted, living our lives to nourish our hearts.

Inclusiveness and non-judgement fortify our personal and collective wellbeing. With loving intention, we can all learn to share, support, connect and unite with one another with a shared sense of purpose. Open-heartedness is a gift to ourselves, each other and our world. As a connecting force, a magic maker, a healer and an amplifier, love touches and enchants us all.

Flourishing together now through love matters more than ever. Living too quickly and often too brashly, with deficits of compassion and loving kindness in our modern world, we human beings can find ourselves weary and hurting, along with our sacred, natural earth. We all need and deserve compassion, tenderness and care. By transforming individualistic 'me' thinking into collective 'us' thinking through the power of love, we will welcome a new, collaborative age together, seeing ourselves not as separate but as deeply, eternally connected.

Let us return to the power of love, grace, and faith in miracles. Let us soften into all possibilities for peace and joy that constantly surround us. Let us choose love and, in choosing love, may we feel more abundant, more beautiful and more alive than ever before.

ACKNOWLEDGEMENTS

This book has brought me more profoundly in touch with the depths of love, held me more accountable than ever before to choosing love, and elevated my desire to live lovingly in ways I could never quite have imagined. This book has expanded my compassion, inspired my gratitude and grown my tenderness for the grace and joy of living. It has also nourished my desire to contribute in some way to the greater blossoming of love and peace on earth.

I would like to express my thanks to all those behind the scenes, assisting to bring this book to life. To my publishers Hardie Grant, especially Sandy Grant, Pam Brewster, Kirstie Grant, Todd Rechner, Marg Bowman and Bernie Gill. To book designer Mietta Yans, for her tremendous creativity and vision, and to editor Allison Hiew, for her ever gentle, wise and loving touch. To graphic artist Meaghan Thomson for her professionalism and attention to detail, and to Mick Smith and his team at Splitting Image for their careful handling of my original artwork.

I thank my family and friends for their constant support and encouragement. I also express heartfelt gratitude and love for my partner, Roberto, with whom life is lived as prayer. For our beautiful, ever-inspiring home, for the companionship of our loved ones and pets, for our pleasure in nature and all the things that bring us bliss – I am fortified and nurtured in the peace of our love.

Exploring love has necessitated deep dives into thoughts and feelings of all kinds, met in my own colourful and rich life experiences in and around writing this book, but also in divine messages I constantly receive from heaven. In nurturing the essence of heaven on earth, it behoves us all to choose love: to see the beauty in things great and small, to nourish and inspire positive and compassionate thinking, and to live heart-centred lives in which all things pivot around love.

Last but not least, thank you, dearest reader, for your time and care. May we choose to know love not only as the energy of life, but as a way of life.

Love, Meredith x

Published in 2021 by Hardie Grant Books,
an imprint of Hardie Grant Publishing

Hardie Grant Books (Melbourne)
Wurundjeri Country
Building 1, 658 Church Street
Richmond, Victoria 3121

Hardie Grant Books (London)
5th & 6th Floors
52–54 Southwark Street
London SE1 1UN

hardiegrantbooks.com

Hardie Grant acknowledges the Traditional Owners of the country on which we
work, the Wurundjeri people of the Kulin nation and the Gadigal people of the
Eora nation, and recognises their continuing connection to the land, waters and
culture. We pay our respects to their Elders past, present and emerging.

Choosing Love
ISBN 978 1 74379 743 3

10 9 8 7 6 5 4 3 2 1

A catalogue record for this
book is available from the
National Library of Australia

Publisher: Pam Brewster
Editor: Allison Hiew
Designer: Mietta Yans
Production Manager: Todd Rechner

Colour reproduction by Splitting Image Colour Studio
Printed in China by Leo Paper Products LTD.

MIX
Paper from
responsible sources
FSC® C020056

The paper this book is printed on is from
FSC®-certified forests and other sources.
FSC® promotes environmentally responsible,
socially beneficial and economically viable
management of the world's forests.